# Praise for the *Tao of Composition*

"I hadn't felt the purity, the rapture until my eyes had widened like a very fresh, warm stream of lilac flowers flowing from the illuminated minds which live through the *Tao of Composition*."

—Michael Piccola

"I pillaged through the dark ages of composition for what seemed like centuries. But then, I was illuminated by Storey and Kantor's *Tao* and have now enlightened thousands with my superior skills of analysis."

—Colby Rogers

"Composition and research papers never clicked for me; I was lost in the abyss of ignorance, until, Storey and Kantor's *Tao of Composition* enlightened me with the brilliance I needed to write my research papers. I am a new woman now."

—Jenni Vaughan

# E-Mail Praise for the *Tao of Composition*

"I just got back from my first English class, and I found out I'm going to have to write a 10-12 page research paper. As scary as that may be, I'm confident that I'll do well on it since I've had experience writing them."

—Carla Cortinas

"I wanted to write and thank you for all the tips you gave to me on my papers because it's really paying off! I have gotten A+'s on my papers, and all my professors asked how I knew how to write so well, and I told them, it was my senior English teacher that inspired me to do my best."

—Maura Slater

"I'm a believer...I knew all through college that there was something about my writing style that was weak, something that was helping me to B's instead of A's. Granted, I was also less mature intellectually. But having taken a few clues from the *Tao*, I can happily say that the first comment on my *Moby Dick* paper for a graduate level course was, 'extremely well-written.' Thanks for the help, guys."

—Joseph Inman

"Oh, yeah, you are right...your papers are going to help us. We already have to do [annotated] bibs."

—Karan Bratton

"I have wanted to let you know about Dan's glowing reports form Denver University about his English class. The teacher raves about his papers, and he was chosen to read one of them in a school-wide English reading assembly. One of the teachers wants him to enter it in a national essay contest. Dan says he learned it all from you. Also, Nick's latest e-mail has a thank you note from a philosophy professor who asked Nick to critique his 700-page novel. I am so glad my sons went to BL and got to have you to light the fire under them for English and writing."

—Colleen Martin

"I just got my first paper back, on which I received an 'A!' Pretty amazing, huh? Thanks for preparing me and affecting my college success no matter how little you or I knew of it."

—Blake Wilson

"Just wanted to thank you for that guide to writing research papers. A few weeks back my Seminar For Television Analysis teacher says that we have to write an annotated bib. So everyone in the class is clueless as to what an annotated bib is, but Ryan and I feel so smart. I also found out that 'annotated bib' must be a BL-coined word because every time I said it, I got an odd look. Not like the normal odd ones but like a confused one. No one shortens bibliography to bib; who knew? So encourage the seniors to use it all the time. Maybe it could be the new word for the year. So anyway, that guide is really saving my life up here, so thanks."

—Jerry Walkup

"I'm here in Austin about to write a paper...and I thought of my good ol' English teacher...and the 'detailed packet on how to write a paper' that I don't have. It's funny because the exact way our professor wants us to write is everything in that packet...so if you could do me a big favor and e-mail it to me, I would greatly appreciate it! Looks like you did your job and prepared me for college, but I'm the dumb-ass that didn't bring that great piece of literature with me. You'll be glad to hear that the reading is overwhelming, but the 'active reading' notes really help a lot."

—Barrett Reeves

"Well, I have to also say thank you because I'm on my second paper and although it isn't research, the *Tao of Composition* methods have come in very handy. It's surprising to know how many people don't know MLA yet; they have copies on reserve in the library, and I feel like a nerd since there is one in my dorm!"

—Vanessa Ferrusca

"Oh, I have to tell you that all my English teachers have loved my writing and my papers thanks to you teaching me how to write so well! I still use this packet you handed out once to help me write papers."

—Marilee Carroll

# Tao of Composition

# Tao of Composition

## The Eight-Fold Path to Analytical Enlightenment

*William Storey & Stuart Kantor*

iUniverse, Inc.

New York  Lincoln  Shanghai

Tao of Composition
The Eight-Fold Path to Analytical Enlightenment

iUniverse, Inc.


For information address:
iUniverse, Inc.
2021 Pine Lake Road, Suite 100
Lincoln, NE 68512
www.iuniverse.com


ISBN: 0-595-28438-8

Printed in the United States of America

Dedicated to:
The students who seek to know what they do not
and understand what they forgot

The authors would like to acknowledge not only those who have written in support of the *Tao*, but also those students who have graciously contributed their works as samples to make this endeavor complete for all future seekers of knowledge. We would also like to acknowledge our English department colleagues whose invaluable contributions to this handbook will help further the cause of intellectual enlightenment.

# Contents

# Introduction

You are about to embark upon the journey of a lifetime. For many, the research paper is an intimidating task; in fact, some even consider it an instrument of evil. However, the guide that follows will help you through the darkness and into the blinding light of analytical enlightenment. What we provide for the eager student is a way or path towards understanding the often-difficult process of constructing a paper. Towards this end, we supply a detailed discussion of each stage in the writing process, including student samples. Each sample represents a student's effort to follow the form and process in the *Tao of Composition*. These students are, like you, attempting to use the enclosed methods of development to hone their composition skills, and their examples should be read with this idea in mind. Yet, their samples do represent hours of hard work and dedication to understanding the process, but these samples are not templates to merely copy or mimic blindly. Instead, they are simply visual aids to help gain a perspective on the process. Keep in mind, writing is a developed discipline and there are no effort-free methods, at least none that are honest. So, following a process produces well-organized and analytically insightful essays that will, with practice, effortlessly flow from your fingertips.

Since all formal papers require a consistent documentation and organizational style, we require that essays be written in objective language and adhere to the guidelines for margins and documentation as found in the *MLA Handbook* and the *Tao of Composition*.

* While Student Samples appear justified in this book, it is purely for publication purposes. Your work should reflect the margins stated in the MLA Handbook.

# Editing Checklist

# Editing Checklist

1.  Do not use 1st or 2nd person references.

    First and/or second person references lend themselves too easily to subjective writing. A research paper is a 100% objective presentation; wherein, the author demonstrates his/her ability to research, logically organize and express without bias the information requested from the instructor.

2.  Do not use past tense when discussing a literary work (unless inside quotes); in general, keep verb tenses consistent.

    Present tense verbs are important because of their impact upon the audience. A story told in the present tense captures and delivers the action with a sense of immediacy; hence, this hint of the dramatic will keep the audience turning the pages. Although it may seem strange to write of historical events and people in the present tense—as if the events are occurring or the people still alive—trust in the present tense's ability to capture the audience without really sounding strange. It is appropriate to use past tense in direct quotes from either your primary or secondary sources.

3.  Avoid passive voice (unless inside quotes).

    Use the active voice; "it is usually more direct and vigorous than the passive" (Strunk 18). As with past tense verbs, passive voice is perfectly acceptable when directly quoting either the primary or secondary sources.

    **Passive Voice**: "There were a great number of Egyptian vessels lying on the ground."

    **Active Voice**: "Egyptian vessels cover the ground."

4.  Avoid vague references.

    Be specific! Colorless, noncommittal language is weak. Understand you are not writing fiction where adjectives and verbs create marvelous images; however, you should always strive to be as specific as possible in all writing—including research papers. State that "the American Revolution, which occurs in 1776, becomes socially relevant to a 21st century

America" rather than "many people today believe the war, which happens in the olden times, has relevance today." State that "Mary Shelley creates a modern myth of man's relationship to the ultimate act of omnipotent power with her novel *Frankenstein*" as opposed to "the author of *Frankenstein* creates a myth." In essence, whenever possible, always prefer the specific to the general and the concrete over the abstract.

5.  Make sure pronouns agree.

    Since we speak incorrectly constantly, it is only logical that students will write this way. For example, it sounds perfectly reasonable to state, "Everyone turned in their homework," when, in fact, the word "everyone" is singular. Therefore, the sentence should read, "Everyone turned in his or her homework." We often hear, "The basketball team won their first game of the season." It should read, "The basketball team won its first game of the season," since the word "team" is singular. When you proofread and edit research papers, double-check pronouns for consistency in singular or plural agreement.

6.  Make sure subjects and verbs agree.

    It is vitally important to the credibility of the paper that elementary grammar be edited and corrected. Since subject/verb agreement is a common mistake, make sure you proofread your sentences carefully. Remember, "Use a singular verb form after *each*, *either*, *everyone*, *everybody*, *neither*, *nobody*, and *someone*" (Strunk 10). This is basic grammar and not as common a speaking mistake as pronoun agreement.

7.  Do not use rhetorical questions.

    Why is it important not to use rhetorical questions? Rhetorical questions make a research paper sound intellectually elementary and emotional. They serve no real purpose except to insight an idea within the reader's imagination that could or could not relate to the intellectual idea you present. Leading the audience through rhetoric is best saved for persuasive essays where you want to bring attention to a specific concern or to highlight an issue for discussion. Research papers are designed to present information in a purely objective style; rhetorical questions are guiding, which edges toward subjectivity.

8. Do not use clichés, overused expressions, jargon, etc.

   In relation to academic papers, clichés, overused expressions, jargon, slang, dialect, etc. all point toward intellectual and critical immaturity. These literary devices are only acceptable in a direct quote from the Primary or Secondary Source. More times than not, if a direct quote from a Primary or Secondary Source contains a cliché or slice of jargon, it is probably not a wonderful quote in the first place.

9. Do not begin a sentence with a quote.

   Beginning a sentence with a quote tells the audience and the instructor one thing: you are depending upon your Primary or Secondary Source information to provide you with original thought. Before any quote, the writer should always construct a dependent or independent clause that introduces a concept, the author and the work or both. Also, preliminary information that subtly segues into the quote is an excellent method of introduction.

10. Do not begin or end a paragraph with a quote.

    It is the writer's job to create effective transitions from the end of one paragraph into the next; the writer should always introduce a quote and analyze it. Therefore, neither the end nor the beginning of subsequent paragraphs contain either a direct quote or paraphrased information. The opening sentence or two of each Body Paragraph should contain information relevant to the appropriate subtopic; in other words, a Thesis Statement of sorts for that Body Paragraph.

11. Do not bold or underline the title.

    When your paper is published some day, then feel free to underline the title or put it in bold or italics or quotation marks or even wingdings if you prefer. Until then, leave it just like the rest of the paper: in 10-12 point type, Times New Roman font. {Check with your instructor for preferred point size and font style.}

12. Do not use quotes in the Thesis Paragraph or Conclusion.

    As you will soon discover, the Thesis Paragraph serves the purpose of introducing the author and title of the Primary Source as well as the General Topic, Supporting Topics and a Thesis Statement. Regardless of the length of the Thesis Paragraph, it is important to remember to assert introductory information based on your objective evaluation of the Primary Source. Do not introduce the Secondary Source in the Thesis or Conclusion.

13. Do not use quotation marks to emphasize words; quotation marks are for information transcribed word for word form the primary or secondary source.

    In the *Austin Powers'* trilogy, Dr. Evil gestures quotation marks to emphasize something to his minion, like the word "laser." This technique is fine for screenplays, poems, short stories, and various forms of feature writing; however, in a research paper it is unnecessary to use quotation marks to emphasize a word or concept.

14. Remember to use a variety of sentence styles: simple, compound, complex, and compound-complex.

    The classic short story *The Sniper* by O'Flaherty uses predominantly simple sentences…short, simple sentences. This is done for dramatic appeal. Rarely is a research paper a drama, although students may become dramatic during the arduous process of researching and writing one. To academically and objectively engage the audience, it is best to mix the sentence styles. When a dramatic point needs emphasis, employ simple sentences. When presenting less dramatic information, switch between styles. However, you do not want to sacrifice clarity for brevity or drama. Remember, academic papers only seek to educate and elucidate the mysteries of human existence found in the language of the Primary or Secondary Sources; construct the foundation, your sentences, with this level of importance.

# Important Definitions

✓ **Sentence**—As William Strunk Jr. and E. B. White state in their classic *The Elements of Style*, "When a sentence is made stronger, it usually becomes shorter. Thus, brevity is a by-product of vigor" (19). However, you do not want to sacrifice analytical depth just to create a short sentence. Brevity, in this case, means creating an economical sentence that still contains all of the necessary analytical elements. Do not string together a series of short, simple sentences and call it brevity. All you will accomplish is a series of redundant concepts, written in staccato fashion that leads to only one simple critical observation.

✓ **General Topic**—Simply, this is the basis of your analysis and states the focus of the Primary Source and, consequently, your paper. Even though it is a General Topic, you do want to narrow it down, so you can limit the idea in the Subtopic section. Instead of the General Topic, Vikings, for example, you would narrow it to research Viking Wedding Ceremonies or Viking Ships: War Ships vs. Travel Ships.

✓ **Subtopics**—This section of your paper outlines how the writer limits the General Topic by creating ideas that define the analytical boundaries for this topic and ultimately the Thesis Statement. These boundaries enable the instructor to understand the focus and limitations of your intellectual exercise, and they create viable topic sentences or concepts for each Body Paragraph.

✓ **Thesis Statement**—This statement is the ultimate statement of purpose and outlines why it is important to understand the intellectual ramifications of the topic and subtopics of the paper.

✓ **Primary Source**—This source is the book, magazine or Internet article that you will use as the basis of your analysis. Your Topic and Subtopics come from this source and your objective is to analyze the socio-political, spiritual or general cultural implications of the work.

✓ **Secondary Sources**—These are additional books, magazines, Internet articles, film documentaries, or even personal interviews, which will support the Primary Source. Secondary Sources are not used to mimic your observation. Like all evidence, this material should validate and extend your observations, so you can transition into the next introduction, concept and quote in the Body Paragraph.

✓ **Sentence Pattern**—This concept applies to the series of sentences in the Body Paragraphs of the Topic and Research papers.
*Topic Paper*: 1–2–3–4–5–3–4–5–3–4–5
*Research Paper*: 1–2–3–4–5–3–4–5–3–4–5–3–4–5–3–4–5

✓ **Pattern of Evidence**–This concept applies to the series of quotes and their origin in the Body Paragraphs of the Topic and Research papers.
*Topic Paper*: Primary–Primary–Primary
*Research Paper*: Primary–Secondary–Primary–Secondary–Primary

# Numbers within the Sentence Pattern

❖ **1**—This number always represents the topic of the Body Paragraph. This topic is also connected to the Subtopic section of the Thesis Paragraph.

❖ **2**—This number always represents the limiting or outlining section of the Body Paragraph. You limit the focus of the topic sentence into three concepts. Just as the General Topic of the Thesis Paragraph is limited by the three Subtopics, so does this limiting sentence provide the three main ideas of the Body Paragraph.

❖ **3**—This number always represents the introduction to the concepts outlined in the number **2** sentence. Look at the sentence pattern for the Body Paragraph; note that each **3** precedes a **4** and each **4** precedes a **5**. Therefore, if you define three concepts in the number **2** sentence then each **3** represents the establishment of those concepts respectively.

❖ **4**—This number always represents the piece of evidence from the Primary or Secondary Sources. This evidence can be paraphrased, summarized or directly quoted. However, each method requires a proper parenthetical citation. If each **3** is an introduction to an outlined concept then each **4** represents a passage from the text that validates and illustrates that concept. Do not restate or summarize the quote as an introduction (**3**) or analysis (**5**). You do not want to document a quote that uses the same language of **3** or **5**; instead, you should strive to find textual evidence that advances the proposed concept found in **3**.

❖ **5**—This number always represents the analysis of **4** and should elaborate on the meaning of the Thesis Statement. Remember, elaborate means to discuss the implications of the textual evidence in relation to the ultimate purpose of your essay or the Thesis Statement. You should look at individual words or phrases when you analyze as a means of providing a sharper focus on the implications to the introduced concept in **3**. Also, the last **5** in the Sentence Pattern will provide a transition into the next Body Paragraph.

# Active Reading

# Active Reading

## Definition:

> ➤ Preliminary process that involves the physical and intellectual engagement of the text—Primary and Secondary Sources.

## Requirements:

> ➤ Required texts
>
> ➤ Pen, pencil or highlighter
>
> ➤ Intellectual curiosity

## Purpose

> ➤ Through a process of highlighting important information, providing insightful comments in the margins, and summarizing major themes, you will successfully develop a close reading of any text. The first step is to highlight information you believe to be important. It is always better to have too much information than not enough; paring the information can be done later. Second, either in the margins of the text or in a separate notebook, summarize or paraphrase the highlighted passages. This process condenses the amount of information from several books and magazines and articles to just an organized notebook, and enables you to internalize the highlighted information, thus making it easier for you to write the paper without any hint of a plagiarized word. Finally, summarize major themes. This way, in whatever manner you choose to code these major themes, when it comes time to compose your opening stages of the paper, you will be highly organized. This is a fantastic way to reduce the natural stress students receive from research papers.

# Brainstorming

# Brainstorming

## Definition:

> ➢ Brainstorming is the first stage in the writing process and provides a vehicle for you to write freely without concern for form.

## Requirements:

> ➢ Required texts
>
> ➢ Notes
>
> ➢ Pen/pencil or word processor
>
> ➢ Intellectual curiosity

## Purpose

> ➢ In this stage, gather all of your active reading notes and concepts for an analysis and begin to establish ideas for the paper. Remember, do not worry about form; just write. The most important thing here is that your brain is working, that it is generating ideas regardless of logical connection to one another. Worry about logic later; for now, simply toss out idea after idea after idea. With enough ideas on paper, discovering patterns from which to pull a General Topic and Subtopics will be easy. Remember to type all of your notes; by establishing a database of all words, phrases and sentences, you will have a language resource to draw from once you start the other stages.

Student Sample

# Sample 1: Brainstorming

Brainstorming

Duality

Rose
- Dimmsdale before death
- Novel's purpose
- Pearl
- Dimmsdale's purpose
- Transcendentalist base theory
- Scaffold
- Imagination
- Human nature
- Intellectual/emotional aspects of human nature
- Town/nature

Transcendentalist Concept:
Duality is the root of romantic and transcendentalist concepts in literature. Beginning with a perspective of humans: people are born naturally innocent and pure, and then are corrupted by the societal establishments. The only way to reach true enlightenment is by returning to the purity of nature and allowing it to purify the corrupt soul. Duality is expressed in the concept that only after innocence is lost can true enlightenment follow.

This concept of romantic duality is displayed throughout the Scarlet Letter in its themes, symbols and characters.

Theme:
The theme of the Scarlet Letter is revealed though the stress on the balance of emotional and intellectual awareness: a dual purpose to live a complete, peaceful and harmonious life. Romantic, or American transcendentalist writers portrayed the importance of this life concept by illustrating the necessity and consequence of the lack of that duality. Hawthorne uses these characters to depict extremes, the consequences, and the balance of these two important romantic qualities of the emotion and intellect.

Characters:

Chillingsworth, though his malicious, monomaniacal quest to destroy the soul of Hester's fellow adulterer depicts his journey to unravel a secret depending solely on his intellectual instincts and judgment.

Dimmsdale, on the other hand, represents an emotional and inadvertently spiritual extreme. He is unable to overcome the burden of his sin and, because of this, this emotion blinds him by his lack of reason in his situation.

Pearl represents the romantic duality, which importance is shown by the consequences of wither emotional or intellectual extremes. She is also the chain between the corrupt town and the purity of nature. Pearl, a product of a forbidden affair that is shadowed in guilt, pain, and regret, exemplifies the dual aspects of the purity of nature, and the corruption of the town. Her discomfort and devilish behavior in the town changes as she enters the forest greeted by the flowers and embraced by the animals. This duality, a balance of two extremes personified in Dimmsdale and Chillingsworth, is Pearl's personal until she is released by her father's admittance of his sin.

Symbols:

Hawthorne uses symbols to convey the concept of duality in the Scarlet Letter.

The rose is perhaps the most obvious of symbols representing both beauty and pain. The rose is located alongside the prison door, a portal to the novel, showing its beauty to those entering condemnation; it is again presented in the governor's mansion, an English garden failing in the rough American soil, the beautiful product of a forced and uncomfortable situation, like Pearl.

Hawthorne uses the scaffold to symbolize both humiliation and truth; as Hester is publicly displayed for three hours for her crime of adultery, her true love, Dimmsdale, seven years later, finds truth, redemption and final solace on the same scaffold.

Dimmsdale's confession is also a symbol of duality. Hawthorne describes how, with a pained expression on his face, he asked Hester to help him onto the scaffold to confess; however, when he confesses, he shows an extraordinary sense of relief and peace. This dual presence of pain and peace are displayed by Dimmsdale's expression, and its consequence on the scaffold seven years after he committed and hid his adultery.

# Outline Form

# Outline Form

## Definition:

> Outlining your Topic and Subtopics is the second stage in the writing process and allows you to create a logical progression of ideas for the analysis. Use a standard outline to accomplish your objective.

## Requirements:

> Required text

> Brainstorming notes

> Pen/pencil or word processor

> Intellectual curiosity

## <u>Standard Outline:</u>

General topic statement

I.   First subtopic
   A.   First supporting concept
   B.   Second supporting concept
   C.   Third supporting concept

II.  Second subtopic
   A.   First supporting concept
   B.   Second supporting concept
   C.   Third supporting concept

III. Third subtopic
   A.   First supporting concept
   B.   Second supporting concept
   C.   Third supporting concept

Thesis statement

# Student
# Samples

# Sample 1: Outline

Outline

In the *Scarlet Letter*, Hawthorne employs the concept of Romantic duality to convey the necessity of both positive and negative forces in order to achieve balance through his use of themes, characters and symbols.

I.  The theme of the *Scarlet Letter* illustrates Hawthorne's concept of Romantic duality within the text in order to teach the reader the transcendental philosophy
    A.  The theme of the book has a dual purpose, stressing the importance of the balance of both intellectual and emotional awareness
    B.  The concept of transcendentalism, that enlightenment is only attained through a purity that has been corrupted, is a theme that displays the significance of duality within the novel
    C.  The delicate balance of both the spiritual, inwards self with the aspect of humans that connects to the 'magnetic chain of humanity', a dual purpose, reflects the purpose of the characters in which the novel emphasizes.

II.  Hawthorne's characters, by exemplifying the intellectual and emotional extremes as well as their balance, along with the consequences of not achieving the balance of the positive and negative, depict the concept of Romantic duality as it applies to humans and their natural tendencies.
    A.  Chillingworth represents an intellectual extreme as a man whose sole purpose is a self-centered journey to destroy another man's soul and, in the process, mutates himself into a fiend, a devilish human whose malicious drive consumes his life and, eventually, destroys him
    B.  Dimmesdale represents an inward extreme through him consumption by emotional and spiritual powers within his life, causing him to live in such pain that, even when given an opportunity to escape, his pain blinds him to the internal power that continually punishes him
    C.  Pearl represents a balance of both the purity of nature and the corruption of society; she is torn between the two forces and, by the end of the novel, releases the sin that divides her,

allowing her to become the beautiful symbol of a balanced and harmonious being

III. Hawthorne inserts physical symbols again to convey the essential duality in life, showing the reader what positive and negative can come to represent
   A. The rose, a symbol of both beauty and pain, is present within Hawthorne's novel to infuse the story with the significant concept of Romantic duality and it's balance
   B. The scaffold symbolizes a dual concept of both humiliation, when Hester is being publicly shunned for her sin and the concept of truth, when Dimmesdale finally admits to his sin; the dual purpose of the scaffold, humiliation and truth, works as a continual reminder of duality
   C. Hawthorne, when describing Dimmesdale's confession, notes both his pained expression and his relief regarding his sin; his dual emotions portrays that positive and negative repercussions that follow any action, in this case, a confession that sets his soul free though his unexpected death on the scaffold

The theme, characters and symbols that Hawthorne uses to convey the significance of Romantic duality to teach the reader the consequences of its absence, as well as the freedom gained through its presence.

# Sample 2: Outline

## Transitional Giotto

The famous Italian artist, Giotto di Bondone, brings the Medieval Period to a close by developing new concepts for the fresco style of painting, thus establishing a basis for the prominent painters of the Renaissance Period.

I. Italian painting in the Greek and Byzantine style before and during Giotto's lifetime consists of flat, two-dimensional figures.
   A. Artists use patterns to adorn the borders and garments in their paintings, often including gold lines that stand out; however, these lines create a flatness and unrealism that hinders the feasibility of the practicality of the painting.
   B. Compositional devises help the artist to direct the viewer to the main focus of the painting such as symmetry and centrality that often make the subjects appear unnaturally manipulated and misplaced.
   C. The naturalism that Giotto establishes is mainly based on the ideas of such people as Saint Francis of Assisi.

II. Giotto brings about a more realistic style of painting that discards some old ways of painting and thinking to construct a new way of creating and viewing paintings.
   A. Giotto uses a more naturalistic style in which the images are three-dimensional and have depth and perspective to create a more realistic composition.
   B. The subjects of Giotto's paintings appear more human than previous artists portray, conveying recognizable emotions and features to create a more understandable and personal work of art.
   C. The body language, positioning, and stance of the individuals in the painting direct the viewer's eye in a natural flow to the specific points of focus.

III. As a transitional artist, Giotto influences the painters of the European Renaissance Period through his change of style, thus making Giotto's style apparent in future artists' works.
   A. The first widely known Florentine painter of the Renaissance, Masacio, comes years after Giotto, but not without much influence from Giotto's work and the new style.

B.  Giotto is commissioned to adorn the interior of a church with large frescos and its vaulted ceiling by dividing it into panels and re-creating the Bible narrative as Michelangelo does centuries later.

C.  Many Renaissance artists praise Giotto for the innovations he makes in painting to make painting more reasonable, which is necessary in a time when scientific theories and advancements are becoming more popular.

Before, during, and after the Medieval Period, art is progressively becoming more realistic and understandable to the common man; Giotto takes a big step in changing the style successfully while retaining the inherent dignity that remains with prestigious painting forever.

# Sample 3: Outline

## Objection to Rejection

In her Gothic novel *Frankenstein*, Mary Shelley portrays Victor Frankenstein's monster as an innocent creature who, as a result of paternal and societal rejection, metamorphoses into a murderous fiend.

I.  Initial rejection of creator and rejection of villagers
    a.  Frankenstein intends for his creation to be beautiful but is horrified by its hideousness.
    b.  Frankenstein flees not in fear of injury but in an instinctive fear of the hideous.
    c.  The monster's first experience with society occurs when he enters a village where people do not attempt to communicate with him but instead attack him.

II. Rejection of the De Lacey family
    a.  The monster, aware of his own deformity, decides to present himself to the blind De Lacey and then to the others.
    b.  The blind man accepts the monster in friendship, but when the others see him, they assume he is dangerous and attack.
    c.  After the De Laceys abandon their home, the monster vows revenge on mankind.

III. Final rejection of creator by refusing to create a female
    a.  The monster seeks out Frankenstein and promises to live in isolation and peace if Frankenstein will create a female like him.
    b.  Frankenstein cannot sympathize with the monster simply because of his deformity but agrees to create a mate.
    c.  Frankenstein stops his work because of its repulsiveness; he rips his creation apart in front of the monster's eyes. The monster will spend the rest of his life avenging this final act of rejection.

Frankenstein's monster experiences three progressively devastating levels of rejection based on physical appearance; the denial of the love and acceptance he seeks transforms the monster from an innocent creation into a bitter fiend who vows revenge against mankind.

# Thesis Paragraph

# Thesis Paragraph

## Definition:

- The Thesis paragraph is the third stage and provides the general topic (*What*), subtopics (*How*) and thesis statement (*Why*) for the paper.

## Requirements:

- Required text
- Brainstorming notes
- Standard Outline or Web Diagram
- Pen/pencil or word processor
- Intellectual curiosity

## Purpose

- This paragraph establishes the general and specific guidelines for you and your reader; it also demonstrates your grasp of the topic and ability to present a logical pattern of ideas that you will elaborate on in the Body Paragraphs of the paper.

  *          *          *

- The sample that follows provides the exact requirements for each section of the Thesis Paragraph.

- Pay particular attention to the words in **bold type.**

- Remember to use objective language, a variety of sentence styles and appropriate transitions.

# Basic Thesis Paragraph: What, How and Why

Full Name

Instructor

Class

Day Month Year

Basic Thesis Paragraph [Insert Your Working Title Here]

**WHAT** is the topic? Through your answer, you will:

❖ Establish the **author, title** and **general topic** of the **Primary Source** and paper.

❖ Provide a transition sentence to **define and limit** the General Topic.

**HOW** will the topic be proven? Through your answer you will:

❖ Establish the **first Subtopic** and its general connection to the main topic.

❖ Establish the **second Subtopic** and its general connection to the main topic.

❖ Establish the **third Subtopic** and its general connection to the main topic.

• *Remember, these subtopics will be the basis for the topic sentences in the Body Paragraphs of your paper, so create **key phrases** that will help identify the Subtopics when you produce these Body Paragraphs.*

<u>**WHY**</u> is this topic important? Through your answer, you will present the following:

❖ The last sentence of the Thesis Paragraph is called the **Thesis Statement**; this statement is the **point you will prove in the paper** and provides the logical conclusion given the General Topic and Subtopics.

[**Remember to use appropriate transitions to connect ideas**]

# Student
# Samples

## Sample 1: Thesis Paragraph

In *The Scarlet Letter*, Nathaniel Hawthorne uses a young, Puritan Boston as the setting for a human drama that incorporates the concept of Romantic duality and the necessity of maintaining balance in life. This concept emphasizes the idea that humans are born pure then become corrupt through the imperfect institutions of society, but by working through these imperfections, they may finally achieve enlightenment. Hawthorne draws the theme of *The Scarlet Letter* from the concept of American transcendentalism, emphasizing a dual human nature and a balance essential to a complete life. In addition, Hawthorne incorporates this transcendental idea of duality in his characters, in order to exemplify both the positive and negative ramifications of duality within human life. Finally, Hawthorne's physical symbols become an obvious reminder of the importance of duality as well as its repercussions, communicating to the reader that duality is not only present in the realm of human life, but also in the perfect existence of nature and the imperfect existence of society. By infusing his novel with a complex philosophy based on the notion of Romantic duality, Hawthorne compels the reader to recognize the opposing forces that govern human consciousness, and once perceived, create a balance of these opposites for health, harmony and human connection.

# Sample 2: Thesis Paragraph

### Land and Taos Pueblo Unite

"I Have Killed the Deer," a Taos Pueblo Song, depicts their understanding of the circle of life; more specifically, it shows their understanding of this circle's ability to infuse images of life and death into the workings of the land. The images that tie life and death into the Pueblo's interactions with the land depict the mutual reliance between the Pueblo community and the land. Another aspect of co-dependence between the Taos and the land is the inseparable physical and spiritual connection with the land that incorporates the workings of life and death. Moreover, the Taos Pueblo and the land share mutual responsibility due to the direct interaction each has to the other's continued well-being. The idea that life and death make up a circle of life, which in turn molds the Pueblo's involvement in relation to man's co-dependence on the natural world, provides the balance between man and the land that is necessary for both to survive.

## Sample 3: Thesis Paragraph

### Objection to Rejection

In her Gothic novel *Frankenstein*, Mary Shelley portrays Victor Frankenstein's monster as an innocent creature who, as a result of paternal and societal rejection, metamorphoses into a murderous fiend. The rejection the monster suffers originates from an innate fear of the hideous; humans who look upon his repulsive countenance react in fear and disgust. During the creature's first interactions with humanity, the man who forms him and the inhabitants of the village into which he wanders act instinctively on their fears instead of attempting to communicate with the monster in an effort to learn his desires and intentions. Despite his devastating first encounters with civilization, the monster's nature remains gentle and he performs gracious deeds for the De Lacey family for months before exposing his presence. He first seeks the blind De Lacey, who recognizes his gentleness, but the other family members, influenced by sight, assume he is dangerous and attack before he is able to reveal his noble nature. The monster's last hope for acceptance and contentment lies in a female with the same defects as himself, whom only Frankenstein has the ability to create. Frankenstein agrees to create a female, but the hideousness of his work causes him to tear the body to pieces before the monster's eyes in a final, unforgivable, act of rejection. The monster experiences three progressively devastating levels of rejection based on physical appearance; the denial of the love and acceptance he seeks transforms the monster from an innocent creation into a bitter fiend who vows revenge against mankind.

# Basic Body Paragraph Construction

# Basic Body Paragraph Construction— with evidence—for the Topic Paper

[Remember to use the appropriate transitions to connect ideas]

1. Provide a Subtopic sentence.

2. Provide a sentence to limit and define the Subtopic sentence.

3. Introduce Primary evidence as well as its important concept. [Note: use the necessary punctuation or method to introduce the quote.]

4. Provide direct, paraphrased or summarized evidence from the Primary Source. [Consult your instructor on which method to use for the assignment.]

5. Analyze Primary source information as it relates to the topic and the Thesis Statement or point you wish to prove.

3. Introduce second Primary evidence as well as its important concept. [Note: use the necessary punctuation or method to introduce the quote.]

4. Provide direct, paraphrased or summarized evidence from the Primary Source. [Consult your instructor on which method to use for the assignment.]

5. Analyze Primary Source information as it relates to the topic and the Thesis Statement or point you wish to prove.

3. Introduce Primary evidence as well as its important concept. [Note: use the necessary punctuation or method to introduce the quote.]

4. Provide direct, paraphrased or summarized evidence from the Primary Source. [Consult your instructor on which method to use for the assignment.]

5.  Analyze Primary source information as it relates to the topic and the Thesis Statement or point you wish to prove and transition into the next paragraph.

# Basic Body Paragraph Construction— with evidence—for the Research Paper

[Remember to use the appropriate transitions to connect ideas]

1.  Provide a Subtopic sentence.

2.  Provide a sentence to limit and define the Subtopic sentence.

3.  Introduce Primary evidence as well as its important concept. [Note: use the necessary punctuation or method to introduce the quote.]

4.  Provide direct, paraphrased or summarized evidence from the Primary Source. [Consult your instructor on which method to use for the assignment.]

5.  Analyze Primary source information as it relates to the topic and the Thesis Statement or point you wish to prove.

3.  Introduce Secondary evidence as well as its important concept. [Note: use the necessary punctuation or method to introduce the quote.]

4.  Provide direct, paraphrased or summarized evidence from the Secondary Source. [Consult your instructor on which method to use for the assignment.]

5.  Analyze Secondary Source information as it relates to the topic and the Thesis Statement or point you wish to prove.

3.  Introduce Primary evidence as well as its important concept. [Note: use the necessary punctuation or method to introduce the quote.]

4.  Provide direct, paraphrased or summarized evidence from the Primary Source. [Consult your instructor on which method to use for the assignment.]

5. **Analyze Primary Source information as it relates to the topic and the Thesis Statement or point you wish to prove.**

3. **Introduce Secondary evidence as well as its important concept.** [Note: use the necessary punctuation or method to introduce the quote.]

4. **Provide direct, paraphrased or summarized evidence from the Secondary Source.** [Consult your instructor on which method to use for the assignment.]

5. **Analyze Secondary Source information as it relates to the topic and the Thesis Statement or point you wish to prove.**

3. **Introduce Primary evidence as well as its important concept.** [Note: use the necessary punctuation or method to introduce the quote.]

4. **Provide direct, paraphrased or summarized evidence from the Primary Source.** [Consult your instructor on which method to use for the assignment.]

5. **Analyze Primary Source information as it relates to the topic and the Thesis Statement or point you wish to prove and transition into the next paragraph.**

# Student
# Samples

## Sample 1: Topic Paper Body Paragraph

Nathaniel Hawthorne draws the theme of *The Scarlet Letter* from the concept of American transcendentalism, emphasizing a dual human nature and a balance essential to a complete life. Hawthorne's purpose for the novel stems from the idea of transcendentalism which states that in order to attain enlightenment, natural purity must be corrupt; this transcendental philosophy emphasizes the necessity of two elements: purity then corruption as crucial elements to gain enlightenment. When the governor of Boston attempts to take Pearl from Hester, Dimmesdale, Hester's minister and secret lover, affirms that she is capable of raising this child, the living emblem of her sin, because of the valuable lesson she continually learns from her enlightenment: "God gave her the child, and gave her, too, an instinctive knowledge of its nature and requirements [...] which no other mortal can posses" (Hawthorne 104). Hester's purity dissolves after she commits adultery with Dimmesdale; however, the knowledge she gains through this sin wields her into an enlightened and conscientious mother and educator for the young child. The theme of *The Scarlet Letter*, with its basis in the transcendental philosophy, has a dual purpose, highlighting the importance of both an intellectual and emotional awareness through the outcomes of the point at which these two capacities fail; with this importance, Hawthorne introduces the reader to his purpose, despite vague narration: "It [the book] may serve...to symbolize some sweet moral blossom, that may be found along the track, or relieve the darkening close of a tale of human frailty and sorrow" (Hawthorne 46). The author uses this "tale of human frailty and sorrow," to convey the human pain and suffering which surfaces from a denial of this indispensable truth. Through the theme, Hawthorne notes the delicate balance of both the inward, spiritual reflection, and the external connection to humanity as a "magnetic chain;" the character's personalities and actions reflect Hawthorne's belief in humans' dual purpose: a responsibility to both the inner self and the outer self. In regard to Dimmesdale's confession, the narrator states that "[a]mong the many morals which press upon us from the poor minister's miserable experience, we put only this into a sentence: 'Be true! Be true! Be true! Show freely to the world, if not your worst, yet some trait whereby the worst may be inferred!'" (Hawthorne 236). When the narrator recounts the events that take place on the scaffold, he presents a statement to assess the theme of the novel: the concept that humans must be true to their own nature, an emotional and spiritual responsibility in order to connect with the rest of humanity, their outward responsibility.

## Sample 2: Topic Paper Body Paragraph

Painting in the Medieval Period, like most art before the Renaissance enlightenment, is not created for the common man; thus most of these old paintings are not easy identifiable to true human life, mainly because of their unrealistic appearance. The lack of realism spawns from the artists' use of flat patterns in large areas, managing compositional devices poorly, and the under-abundance of naturalist ideas. In response to viewing the new realistic style of Giotto, James Snyder declares, "Gone are the gold lines that are usually shot through the costumes and the crisp linear patterns for the draperies" (460). The patterns artists use to adorn the borders and garments in their paintings create a deceptive perspective that hinders the feasibility and practicality of the paintings; Giotto abandons this technique to create three-dimensionality in his works. Compositional devices often enhance a work of art; however, in the Medieval Period, compositional devices impede the plausibility of the subject as an appropriate depiction of the truth: "Giotto avoids such obvious compositional devices as symmetry and centrality" (Snyder 463). While compositional devices often direct the viewer to the desired subject, such noticeable methods often manipulate and misplace the subject beyond the reach of logical arrangement. New ideas arise during Giotto's lifetime that influence the change in style representative of his paintings; for example, "the naturalism of his paintings echoes the sentiments expressed by Saint Francis of Assisi, who made religion a simple, everyday experience that was emotionally appealing to the common man" (Snyder 460). Naturalism is the essential idea that Giotto strives to establish in his paintings so that art, like religion, can relate to and interest the common man.

# Sample 3: Topic Paper Body Paragraph

Despite the creature's innocent intentions in his first interactions with civilization, humans who behold his frightening countenance react in fright and horror. The inhabitants of the first village into which he wanders, as well as the man who forms him, know nothing of the creature's intentions or desires; they act on instinctive fear of the deformed appearance without attempting to communicate with the monster. Instead of triumph, Victor Frankenstein's reaction is one of shock as he accomplishes his aspiration to create life from dead material:

> His limbs were in proportion, and I had selected his features as beautiful. Beautiful! Great God! His yellow skin scarcely covered the work of muscles and arteries beneath; his hair was of a lustrous black, and flowing; his teeth of a pearly whiteness; but these luxuriances only formed a more horrid contrast with his watery eyes, that seemed almost of the same colour as the dun-white sockets in which they were set, his shriveled complexion and straight black lips. (Shelley 42)

Before his moment of achievement, Frankenstein's obsession with his project blinds him to its consequences, but now he can no longer deny the outcome of his actions: his creation is not an accomplishment to proclaim but a monstrosity to fear. Frankenstein now desires escape from his hideous creation and flees not in fear of injury, for the monster makes no aggressive moves; his fear stems from the monster's deformity: "No mortal could support the horror of that countenance. A mummy again endued with animation could not be so hideous as that wretch. I had gazed on him while unfinished; he was ugly then, but when those muscles and joints were rendered capable of motion, it became a thing such as even Dante could not have conceived" (Shelley 43). Before animating the creature, Frankenstein cannot foresee the effect that life will have on an already unsightly form; the result of animation is a living monster whose form is horrible beyond his creator's imagination. Frankenstein would desire recognition for the creation of a beautiful being, and a society prejudiced against the hideous would welcome an attractive creature; however, the creature is not beautiful, and society immediately rejects him: "I [the monster] had hardly set my foot within the door before the children shrieked, and one of the women fainted. The whole village was roused; some fled, some attacked me, until, grievously bruised by stones and many other kinds of missile weapons, I escaped to the open country...miserable...from the barbarity of man" (Shelley 91). The monster enters the village innocently seeking nourishment, but the villagers, due to his horrifying countenance, assume he is dangerous and attack without attempting to discover his intentions.

## Sample 4: Research Paper Body Paragraph

The images that the Taos Pueblo use in their songs and mythology tie life and death to their interactions with the land. Furthermore the Pueblo song, *I have Killed the Deer*, depicts the mutual reliance between the Taos Pueblo community and the resources that stem from the land, exploring the cycle of life and death and emphasizing the co-reliance between the land and Taos Pueblos. The singer of the deer song provides an image that strongly exhibits the mutual reliance the Pueblo people have to the land: "In my life I have needed death/So my life can be"(8-9). This statement highlights the mutual reliance between the Pueblos and the land by describing a simple cycle of life and death founded by the land but left up to the Pueblos, as people, to complete and understand. Moreover, Leslie Silko provides an example of mutual reliance between the land and Pueblo community when she refers to a short story in an attempt to respond to an interview recorded by Thomas Irmer: "White cow, the magic cow, and she would give them enough milk to take care of the people. They must never take too much" (3). This story emphasizes the reliance Taos Pueblos have on the land to provide life-sustaining nourishment and consequently, the earth's reliance on the people to use its resources correctly. Another more specific reliance on the land occurs when the Pueblo poet talks about killing the grasshoppers, deer, and the plants to sustain their life (1-7). Again the cycle of life and death shows the Pueblo's reliance on a food source and the land's reliance on consumption of resources to continue the natural movement of all life towards death, thus ensuring new life in a never-ending circle. Another statement that highlights the reliance Pueblos have on the land comes from Nelson J. Cordova's speech on water and growth issues around New Mexico: "The problem subsided when everyone realized there was no water to fight over"(1). This simple revelation states how much people rely on the resources of the land and again the land relies on the people to use its resources wisely and not abuse what they are given because the earth does not have limitless recourses. Finally, the most vivid piece of imagery in *I Have Killed the Deer* emphasizes a mutual reliance on the land and the cycle of life and death that comes from this special connection: "The earth receives my body/And gives it to the plants"(12-13). This image more completely explains the active reliance of the land; Taos Pueblos return their bodies to the land in order for the Pueblos to give back what the land has provided so that all life can be renewed.

# Topic Paper

# Topic Paper

## Definition:

- The Topic Paper is the fifth stage in the composition process and provides a detailed analysis of the Primary Source.

## Requirements:

- The following sample provides the exact requirements for each section of the Topic Paper.

- Pay particular attention to the words in **bold type.**

- Remember to use objective language, a variety of sentence styles, appropriate transitions, and proper parenthetical citations.

# Topic Paper Construction

Full Name

Instructor

Class

Day Month Year

Title for the Paper

**Topic Paper:** Stage five enables you to create a complete analysis of the Primary Source.

<u>Thesis Paragraph</u>: This introductory paragraph of your paper should explore the following questions: *Note—<u>Do not</u> type the questions.*

<u>WHAT</u> is the topic?

❖ Establish the author title and general topic of the Primary Source and paper.

❖ Provide a transition sentence to define and limit the General Topic.

<u>HOW</u> will the topic be proven?

❖ Establish the **first Subtopic** and its general connection to the main topic.

❖ Establish the **second Subtopic** and its general connection to the main topic.

❖ Establish the **third Subtopic** and its general connection to the main topic.

- *Remember these Subtopics will be the basis for the topic sentences in the Body Paragraphs of your paper, so create **key phrases** that will help identify the Subtopics when you produce these Body Paragraphs.*

<u>WHY</u> is this topic important?

- ❖ The last sentence of the Thesis Paragraph is called the Thesis Statement; this statement is the point you will prove in the paper and provides the logical conclusion given the General Topic and Subtopics.

<u>First Body Paragraph</u>:

1. Provide a Subtopic sentence.

2. Provide a sentence to limit and define the Subtopic sentence.

3. Introduce Primary evidence as well as its important concept. [Note: use the necessary punctuation or method to introduce the quote.]

4. Provide direct, paraphrased or summarized evidence from the Primary Source. [Consult your instructor on which method to use for the assignment.]

5. Analyze Primary source information as it relates to the topic and the Thesis Statement or point you wish to prove.

3. Introduce Primary evidence as well as its important concept. [Note: use the necessary punctuation or method to introduce the quote.]

4. Provide direct, paraphrased or summarized evidence from the Primary Source. [Consult your instructor on which method to use for the assignment.]

5. Analyze Primary Source information as it relates to the topic and the Thesis Statement or point you wish to prove and transition into the next paragraph.

3.  Introduce Primary evidence as well as its important concept. [Note: use the necessary punctuation or method to introduce the quote.]

4.  Provide direct, paraphrased or summarized evidence from the Primary Source. [Consult your instructor on which method to use for the assignment.]

5.  Analyze Primary Source information as it relates to the topic and the Thesis Statement or point you wish to prove and transition into the next paragraph.

<u>Second Body Paragraph:</u>

1.  Provide a Subtopic sentence.

2.  Provide a sentence to limit and define the Subtopic sentence.

3.  Introduce Primary evidence as well as its important concept. [Note: use the necessary punctuation or method to introduce the quote.]

4.  Provide direct, paraphrased or summarized evidence from the Primary Source. [Consult your instructor on which method to use for the assignment.]

5.  Analyze Primary Source information as it relates to the topic and the Thesis Statement or point you wish to prove.

3.  Introduce Primary evidence as well as its important concept. [Note: use the necessary punctuation or method to introduce the quote.]

4.  Provide direct, paraphrased or summarized evidence from the source. [Consult your instructor on which method to use for the assignment.

5.  Analyze Primary Source information as it relates to the topic and the Thesis Statement or point you wish to prove.

3. Introduce Primary evidence as well as its important concept. [Note: use the necessary punctuation or method to introduce the quote.]

4. Provide direct, paraphrased or summarized evidence from the source. [Consult your instructor on which method to use for the assignment.]

5. Analyze Primary source information as it relates to the topic and the Thesis Statement or point you wish to prove and transition into the next paragraph.

Third Body Paragraph:

1. Provide a Subtopic sentence.

2. Provide a sentence to limit and define the Subtopic sentence.

3. Introduce Primary evidence as well as its important concept. [Note: use the necessary punctuation or method to introduce the quote.]

4. Provide direct, paraphrased or summarized evidence from the Primary Source. [Consult your instructor on which method to use for the assignment.]

5. Analyze Primary Source information as it relates to the topic and the Thesis Statement or point you wish to prove.

3. Introduce Primary evidence as well as its important concept. [Note: use the necessary punctuation or method to introduce the quote.]

4. Provide direct, paraphrased or summarized evidence from the Primary Source. [Consult your instructor on which method to use for the assignment.]

5.  Analyze Primary Source information as it relates to the topic and the Thesis Statement or point you wish to prove.

3.  Introduce Primary evidence as well as its important concept. [Note: use the necessary punctuation or method to introduce the quote.]

4.  Provide direct, paraphrased or summarized evidence from the source. [Consult your instructor on which method to use for the assignment.]

5.  Analyze Primary Source information as it relates to the topic and the Thesis Statement or point you wish to prove and transition into the next paragraph.

Conclusion:

❖  Reassert the **Thesis Statement** of the paper.

❖  Review the strongest supporting examples from the **Thesis Paragraph** of the paper.

❖  **Do not** introduce anything new in the conclusion.

## Works Cited

Insert the bibliographic reference from the Primary and Secondary Sources in alphabetical order.

*Note: You must consult the MLA handbook to correctly format the reference for your source.*

# Student
# Samples

# Sample 1: Topic Paper

The Concept of Romantic Duality as it Appears in *The Scarlet Letter*

In *The Scarlet Letter*, Nathaniel Hawthorne uses a young, Puritan Boston as the setting for a human drama that incorporates the concept of Romantic duality and the necessity of maintaining balance in life. This concept emphasizes the idea that humans are born pure then become corrupt through the imperfect institutions of society, but by working through these imperfections, they may finally achieve enlightenment. Hawthorne draws the theme of *The Scarlet Letter* from the concept of American transcendentalism, emphasizing a dual human nature and a balance essential to a complete life. In addition, Hawthorne incorporates this transcendental idea of duality in his characters, in order to exemplify both the positive and negative ramifications of duality within human life. Finally, Hawthorne's physical symbols become an obvious reminder of the importance of duality as well as its repercussions, communicating to the reader that duality is not only present in the realm of human life, but also in the perfect existence of nature and the imperfect existence of society. By infusing his novel with a complex philosophy based on the notion of Romantic duality, Hawthorne compels the reader to recognize the opposing forces that govern human consciousness, and once perceived, create a balance of these opposites for health, harmony and human connection.

Nathaniel Hawthorne draws the theme of *The Scarlet Letter* from the concept of American transcendentalism, emphasizing a dual human nature and a balance essential to a complete life. Hawthorne's purpose for the novel stems from the idea of transcendentalism which states that in order to attain enlightenment, natural purity must be corrupt; this transcendental philosophy emphasizes the necessity of two elements: purity then corruption as crucial elements to gain enlightenment. When the governor of Boston attempts to take Pearl from Hester, Dimmesdale, Hester's minister and secret lover, affirms that she is capable of raising this child, the living emblem of her sin, because of the valuable lesson she continually learns from her enlightenment: "God gave her the child, and gave her, too, an instinctive knowledge of its nature and requirements [...] which no other mortal can posses" (Hawthorne 104). Hester's purity dissolves after she commits adultery with Dimmesdale; however, the knowledge she gains through this sin wields her into an enlightened and conscientious mother and educator for the young child. The theme of *The Scarlet Letter*, with its basis in the transcendental philosophy, has a dual purpose, highlighting the importance of both an intellectual and emotional awareness through the outcomes of the point at which these two capacities fail; with this importance, Hawthorne introduces the reader to his purpose, despite vague narration: "It [the book] may serve...to symbolize some sweet moral blossom, that may be found along the track, or relieve the darkening close of a tale of human frailty and sorrow" (Hawthorne 46). The author uses this "tale of human frailty and sorrow," to convey the twofold message of the book, portraying the human pain and suffering which surfaces from a denial of this indispensable truth. Through the theme, Hawthorne notes the delicate balance of both the inward, spiritual reflection, and the external connection to humanity as a "magnetic chain;" the character's personalities and actions reflect Hawthorne's belief in humans' dual purpose: a responsibility to both the inner self and the outer self. In regard to Dimmesdale's confession, the narrator states that "[a] mong the many morals which press upon us from the poor minister's miserable experience, we put only this into a sentence: 'Be true! Be true! Be true! Show freely to the world, if not your worst, yet some trait whereby the worst may be inferred!'" (Hawthorne 236). When the narrator recounts the events that take place on the scaffold, he presents a statement to assess the theme of the novel: the concept that humans must be true to their own nature, an emotional and spiritual responsibility in order to connect with the rest of humanity, their outward responsibility.

Hawthorne's characters, by exemplifying the intellectual extremes, emotional extremes, the perfection of balance, and the consequences of not achieving equilibrium, depict the idea of Romantic duality as it applies to humans and their natural tendencies. Throughout the novel, Hawthorne emphasizes the negative aspects of the lack of balance in characters' lives by highlighting the ramifications of their actions, rather than the often-negligible positive repercussions. Roger Chillingworth, a man whose sole purpose throughout the novel is an egotistical determination to destroy another man's soul, embodies the intellectual extreme, which results from a lack of balance, mutating himself into a fiend whose malicious drive consumes his life and eventually leads to his destruction. Upon his arrival to the town, Chillingworth reunites with Hester, a now public symbol of ignominy, and tells her of his quest: "...few things hidden from the man who devotes himself earnestly and unreservedly to the solution of a mystery [...] I shall seek this man, as I have sought truth in books [...] Sooner or later, he must needs be mine!"

(Hawthorne 70). Chillingworth declares his unswerving pursuit of Hester's lover in the beginning of the novel, and as the story progresses over seven years, the reader experiences his rejection of humanity and his monomaniacal quest of destruction, illustrating the hideous consequences of a man who turns to darkness through his consumption by a singular purpose in life. Conversely, Dimmesdale represents an inward extreme whereby his emotional and spiritual powers engulf his reason, causing him to live in such pain that, even when given opportunity to escape, his suffering blinds him to the internal powers that punish him for his sin. The author expresses that, while Hester's public humiliation prepares her for the extinction of her sin, Dimmesdale "was broken down by long and exquisite suffering; that his mind was darkened and confused by the very remorse which harrowed it; that between fleeing as an avowed criminal, and remaining as a hypocrite, conscience might find it hard to strike a balance [...] the breach which guilt has once made into the human soul is never, in this mortal state, repaired" (Hawthorne 184). While Hester undergoes the preparation to disregard her sin after seven years of public torment, Dimmesdale, whose pain and regret blind him from all reason, is unable to accept an escape because his private pain cannot be left behind by the simple act of changing physical locations. Finally, Pearl represents the dual existence of both the purity of nature and the corruption of society; these two forces pull her in different directions and when this divergence ends, she becomes the beautiful symbol of a balanced and harmonious human being. When describing Pearl, the author states "that little creature, whose innocent life had sprung, by the inscrutable decree of Providence, a lovely and immortal flower, out of the rank luxuriance of a guilty passion" (Hawthorne 81). Pearl is fundamentally pure at birth, according to transcendentalism; however, she is the innocent product of her parent's hideous sin of adultery, which illustrates her dual nature in the novel until the end of the book when she reconnects with humanity.

Throughout the novel, Hawthorne inserts physical symbols to convey the presence of duality in all aspects of life, including nature, human instinct, and society. Through these obvious symbols, Hawthorne succeeds in keeping the twofold purpose of human existence present throughout the duration of the novel, where the rose, Hawthorne's most frequent symbol of duality, signifies beauty and pain, a concept that infuses the story with the necessity of balance. As the narrator relates the importance of the prison in a Puritan town, he emphasizes not only its paradoxical existence, but also the presence of a rose bush at its threshold, stating "on one side of the portal...was a wild rose-bush, covered in this month of June, with its delicate gems, which might be imagined to offer their fragrance and fragile beauty to the prisoner as he went in, and to the condemned criminal as he came forth to his doom" (Hawthorne 46). The rose's dual purpose, offering the sight of beauty to the condemned, signifies the novel's dual theme as it applies to the perfection of nature. The scaffold is another tangible sign of duality, representing both humiliation, when Hester bears a public condemnation, and redemption, which Dimmesdale achieves when he finally admits his sin in the same location; the purpose of the scaffold, with its position of prominence within the town, works as an incessant reminder of consequences of the imbalance that the characters personify. When Dimmesdale ascends the scaffold to confess and find release from his sin, he declares "at last!—I stand upon the spot where, seven years since, I should have stood; [...] Lo, the scarlet letter which Hester wears! [...] It hath cast a lurid gleam of awe and horrible repugnance round about her. But there stood one in the midst of you, at whose brand of sin and infamy ye have not shuddered" (Hawthorne 231-2). At Hester's confession on the scaffold, she becomes the symbol of ignominy within the community, finding no redemption in the act of confession; however, as Dimmesdale confesses his sin on the scaffold, his profession frees him from the silent torture that weakens him, allowing a final discovery of peace before his death; Hester's humiliation and Dimmesdale's redemption on the scaffold allow it to remain a public image of duality which is forever present within the Puritan society of the novel. When describing Dimmesdale's confession, Hawthorne notes both his pained facial expression and his imminent relief regarding the public deliverance from his sin; as these two emotions exist simultaneously, they come to symbolize the positive and negative repercussions that follow any action, in this case, a confession that although painful, liberates Dimmesdale's soul: "it was a ghastly look with which he regarded them [Hester and Pearl]; but there was something at once tender and strangely triumphant in it" (Hawthorne 229). This contorted, yet victorious gaze that he directs to Hester and Pearl signifies the dual emotion that the minister possesses, both a salubrious and malignant reaction, illustrating the presence of Romantic duality within natural human instincts to infer the beneficial and harmful results of Dimmesdale's sin.

In his novel, Hawthorne conveys the significance of Romantic duality to teach the reader the consequences of its absence, as well as the freedom of its presence. The theme of *The Scarlet Letter* establishes itself through emphasis of Romantic duality and the concept of American transcendentalism: humans are born pure then become corrupt through the imperfect institutions of society, but by working through these imperfections, they may finally achieve enlightenment. Hawthorne also uses his characters to personify the consequences of the absence of balance, which depict the concept of duality as it applies to humanity. Finally, Hawthorne's physical symbols work as a constant reminder of the existence of duality in all aspects of life, society, and human inclination; the use of Romantic duality throughout the novel shows what Hawthorne is truly attempting to covey to the reader the idea that life is the balance of opposing forces, and that without both elements, only a plethora of dissatisfaction results.

## Works Cited

Hawthorne, Nathaniel. *The Scarlet Letter*. Bantam Dell: New York, New York, 1986.

# Sample 2: Topic Paper

## Transitional Giotto

James Snyder's *Medieval Art* recalls the famous Italian artist, Giotto di Bondone, bringing the Medieval Period to a close by developing new concepts for the fresco style of painting, thus establishing a basis for the prominent painters of the Renaissance Period. Giotto combines old ideas with new techniques, consequently creating a style more characteristic of legendary Renaissance painters. Italian paintings in the old Greek and Byzantine styles before and during Giotto's lifetime consist of flat, two-dimensional figures. Giotto brings about a more realistic style of painting that discards several old ways of painting and thinking in an effort to construct a new way of creating and viewing paintings. As a transitional artist between the Middle Ages and the Renaissance, Giotto influences the painters of the European Renaissance Period through his change of style, thus making Giotto's style apparent in future artists' works. Before, during, and after the Medieval Period, art is progressively becoming more realistic and understandable to the common man; Giotto is one of many painters to take a big step towards changing the style successfully while retaining the inherent dignity that forever remains with prestigious painting.

Painting in the Medieval Period, like most art before the Renaissance enlightenment, is not created for the common man; thus most of these old paintings are not easy identifiable to true human life, mainly because of their unrealistic appearance. The lack of realism spawns from the artists' use of flat patterns in large areas, managing compositional devices poorly, and the under-abundance of naturalist ideas. In response to viewing the new realistic style of Giotto, James Snyder declares, "Gone are the gold lines that are usually shot through the costumes and the crisp linear patterns for the draperies" (460). The patterns artists use to adorn the borders and garments in their paintings create a deceptive perspective that hinders the feasibility and practicality of the paintings; Giotto abandons this technique to create three-dimensionality in his works. Compositional devices often enhance a work of art; however, in the Medieval Period, compositional devices impede the plausibility of the subject as an appropriate depiction of the truth: "Giotto avoids such obvious compositional devices as symmetry and centrality" (Snyder 463). While compositional devices often direct the viewer to the desired subject, such noticeable methods often manipulate and misplace the subject beyond the reach of logical arrangement. New ideas arise during Giotto's lifetime that influence the change in style representative of his paintings; for example, "the naturalism of his paintings echoes the sentiments expressed by Saint Francis of Assisi, who made religion a simple, everyday experience that was emotionally appealing to the common man" (Snyder 460). Naturalism is the essential idea that Giotto strives to establish in his paintings so that art, like religion, can relate to and interest the common man.

In a quest to portray the subjects exactly as they are in reality, Giotto develops a new style of painting that incorporates both old and new ideas and techniques. To achieve realism, Giotto uses depth and perspective, recognizable human emotions, and figures' body language and posture. The first step in creating a believable atmosphere is to create proper perspective; Mr. Snyder states that Giotto institutes "a new sense of space [...in which] the three-dimensional qualities of the figures are powerfully stated [...] evoking the qualities of objects we wish to touch as large rounded volumes, as if they were sculptures and no longer flat patterns" (460). The composition is becoming a real world in which a sense of space forms a reasonable scene that people perceive as an accurate depiction of reality. Once Giotto establishes the atmosphere, he paints people in an innovative style; "Human emotions are now registered; a new warmth and intimacy are projected. Real people are placed before our eyes" (Snyder 460). The work of art is now becoming more personal with subjects that experience everyday issues and have feelings; thus breaking away from the standard mug shot pose for portraits and biblical scenes. In contrast to the recognizable compositional devises of earlier times to appropriately direct the viewer's attention, Mr. Snyder affirms, "Giotto controls our attention span through the subtle psychology of directional focus of all figures [...with the] figures closing the compositional field" (464). The more natural flow to specific points of focus in Giotto's paintings makes for a more peaceful composition that is more pleasing to look at than previous works of art that lack appropriate harmony.

Giotto's revolutionary painting techniques became some of the recognizable characteristics of the European Renaissance that follows shortly after his death. Proof of Giotto's influence lies in the first famous Italian Renaissance artist, the Sistine Chapel masterpiece, and the concepts of various legendary artists' of the Renaissance. Although Giotto is not technically is not a part of the Renaissance period, Snyder titles him "the precursor of Masaccio, the first great Renaissance painter in Florence"

(460). The innovative style and ideas of Giotto immediately influence artists in Italy, such as Masaccio, which spawns the beginning of a new era in artistic endeavors. Giotto receives a commission to paint the interior of a chapel "with a vaulted ceiling [...with] Giotto's task to articulate the barren into an elaborate gallery [...and he divided the sidewalls [...to paint] a sequence of narratives" (Snyder 460,462). The pictorial Bible narratives Giotto paints in his chapel job are the foundation for the Sistine Chapel that Michelangelo paints centuries later; even the procedure by which Giotto divides areas into block sections resembles the layout of the later chapel. Numerous other artists born after the Middle Ages appreciate the transformation by Giotto: "He was praised by Dante as a leader in the arts," and "Vasari named him the first truly 'modern' artist to break from the 'crude manner of the Greeks'" (Snyder 460). Artists' and writers praise Giotto for the innovations he makes in painting to make painting more reasonable, which is necessary in a time when scientific theories and advancements are becoming more popular.

Before, during, and after the Medieval Period, art is progressively becoming more realistic and understandable to the common man; Giotto is one of many painters to take a big step towards changing the style successfully while retaining the inherent dignity that forever remains with prestigious painting. Creating new ideas with old techniques and subjects, Giotto creates an innovative style that is more realistic than that of previous paintings. He paves the way for Renaissance artists, which is noticeable in comparing his work with that of famous Renaissance painters; thus making him a legendary transitional artist.

## Works Cited

Snyder, James. Medieval Art. Harry N. Abrams, Inc.: New York, 1989.

# Sample 3: Topic Paper

## Objection to Rejection

In her Gothic novel *Frankenstein*, Mary Shelley portrays Victor Frankenstein's monster as an innocent creature who, as a result of paternal and societal rejection, metamorphoses into a murderous fiend. The rejection the monster suffers originates from an innate fear of the hideous; humans who look upon his repulsive countenance react in fear and disgust. During the creature's first interactions with humanity, the man who forms him and the inhabitants of the village into which he wanders act instinctively on their fears instead of attempting to communicate with the monster in an effort to learn his desires and intentions. Despite his devastating first encounters with civilization, the monster's nature remains gentle and he performs gracious deeds for the De Lacey family for months before exposing his presence. He first seeks the blind De Lacey, who recognizes his gentleness, but the other family members, influenced by sight, assume he is dangerous and attack before he is able to reveal his noble nature. The monster's last hope for acceptance and contentment lies in a female with the same defects as himself, whom only Frankenstein has the ability to create. Frankenstein agrees to create a female, but the hideousness of his work causes him to tear the body to pieces before the monster's eyes in a final, unforgivable, act of rejection. The monster experiences three progressively devastating levels of rejection based on physical appearance; the denial of the love and acceptance he seeks transforms the monster from an innocent creation into a bitter fiend who vows revenge against mankind.

Despite the creature's innocent intentions in his first interactions with civilization, humans who behold his frightening countenance react in fright and horror. The inhabitants of the first village into which he wanders, as well as the man who forms him, know nothing of the creature's intentions or desires; they act on instinctive fear of the deformed appearance without attempting to communicate with the monster. Instead of triumph, Victor Frankenstein's reaction is one of shock as he accomplishes his aspiration to create life from dead material:

> His limbs were in proportion, and I had selected his features as beautiful. Beautiful! Great God! His yellow skin scarcely covered the work of muscles and arteries beneath; his hair was of a lustrous black, and flowing; his teeth of a pearly

whiteness; but these luxuriances only formed a more horrid contrast with his watery eyes, that seemed almost of the same colour as the dun-white sockets in which they were set, his shriveled complexion and straight black lips. (Shelley 42)

Before his moment of achievement, Frankenstein's obsession with his project blinds him to its consequences, but now he can no longer deny the outcome of his actions: his creation is not an accomplishment to proclaim but a monstrosity to fear. Frankenstein now desires escape from his hideous creation and flees not in fear of injury, for the monster makes no aggressive moves; his fear stems from the monster's deformity: "No mortal could support the horror of that countenance. A mummy again endued with animation could not be so hideous as that wretch. I had gazed on him while unfinished; he was ugly then, but when those muscles and joints were rendered capable of motion, it became a thing such as even Dante could not have conceived" (Shelley 43). Before animating the creature, Frankenstein cannot foresee the effect that life will have on an already unsightly form; the result of animation is a living monster whose form is horrible beyond his creator's imagination. Frankenstein would desire recognition for the creation of a beautiful being, and a society prejudiced against the hideous would welcome an attractive creature; however, the creature is not beautiful, and society immediately rejects him: "I [the monster] had hardly set my foot within the door before the children shrieked, and one of the women fainted. The whole village was roused; some fled, some attacked me, until, grievously bruised by stones and many other kinds of missile weapons, I escaped to the open country...miserable...from the barbarity of man" (Shelley 91). The monster enters the village innocently seeking nourishment, but the villagers, due to his horrifying countenance, assume he is dangerous and attack without attempting to discover his intentions.

Despite his devastating first encounter with civilization, the monster's nature remains gentle and he performs gracious deeds for the De Lacey family for months; when he reveals his presence, however, the De Laceys reject him on sight. The blind De Lacey, whom the monster seeks first, recognizes his gentleness, but the other family members, influenced by sight, perceive him as dangerous and attack him before he can demonstrate his noble nature. Scarred from his previous treatment by humans, the monster refrains from immediately presenting himself to the De Laceys and spends time studying their behavior; during this time he discovers the reason for his previous rejection and the importance of verbal communication:

> I had admired the perfect forms of my cottagers...but how was I terrified when I viewed myself in a transparent pool! At first I started back, unable to believe that it was indeed I who was reflected in the mirror; and when I became fully convinced that I was in reality the monster that I am, I was filled with the bitterest sensations of despondence and mortification....I formed in my imagination a thousand pictures of presenting myself to them, and their reception of me. I imagined that they would be disgusted, until, by my gentle demeanour and conciliating words, I should first win their favour and afterwards their love. (Shelley 98-100)

Fully aware of his unnatural physical deformity and the effect it has on humans, the monster decides to present himself to and establish a friendship with the blind father, who will then be able to act as a mediator between him and the rest of the family; however, the creatures plan takes an unfortunate turn as the young De Laceys return in the midst of their first meeting and attack him. The monster's dream of acceptance shatters when the family he has loved and assisted, unseen, for many months rejects him on sight; in response, he swears revenge against mankind but later, "when I considered what had passed at the cottage, I could not help believing that I had been too hasty in my conclusions....It was apparent my conversation had interested the father in my behalf, and I was a fool in having exposed my person to the horror of his children....I resolved to return to the cottage, seek the old man, and by my representations win him to my party" (Shelley 122). The creature accepts blame for his violent eviction from the cottage in hope for a second chance to convey his desire for friendship and compassion, but the family has fled their cottage forever. The monster describes the devastating effect of this one act of rejection on his once loving nature: "For the first time the feelings of revenge and hatred filled my bosom, and I did not strive to control them, but...I bent my mind towards injury and death" (Shelley 123). The creature is willing and able to endure the hatred and scorn of unfamiliar people, but the condemnation of a family he loves and generously serves is an act he cannot forgive.

After coming to know the monster through the creature's personal testimony, Frankenstein agrees to create a female; however, the hideousness of his work causes him to tear the body to pieces before the monster's eyes in a final act of rejection. The creature vows to act in peace towards humanity if Frankenstein will make him happy; the promise and then denial of his single request provokes the monster to revenge. While conversing with his creator, the monster describes the agony of living in a world whose inhabitants are unable to accept a creature with his hideous and misshapen form: "Let him [man] live with me in the interchange of kindness, and instead of injury I would bestow every benefit upon him with tears of gratitude at his acceptance. But that cannot be; the human senses are insurmountable barriers to our union" (Shelley 130). The monster abandons all hope of acceptance and friendship from any member of the human race, for he deems the union of human sight and his own repulsiveness impossible; his last hope of acceptance lies in another being with the same defects as himself. Even as he implores Frankenstein's compassion through his personal testimony, however, his hideous form prevents his creator's sympathy: "I [Frankenstein] compassionated him and sometimes felt a wish to console him, but when I looked upon him, when I saw the filthy mass that moved and talked, my heart sickened and my feelings were altered to those of horror and hatred" (Shelley 132). After listening to the monster's life story, Frankenstein now knows him and understands his thoughts, feelings, and desires; however, as at the time the monster's creation, Frankenstein's failure to love results from the monster's physical gruesomeness. The monster's constant pleas eventually lead Frankenstein to agree to create a female, but Frankenstein allows the physical repulsion he feels as he beholds the female's unfinished form to take precedence over his responsibility towards the monster; he "tore to pieces the thing on which I was engaged. The wretch saw me destroy the creature on whose future existence he depended for happiness, and with a howl of devilish despair and revenge, withdrew" (Shelley 151). With his last dream of companionship destroyed, the monster vows revenge on the man who carelessly created life and then denied the means to enjoy it.

Frankenstein's monster endures three progressively demoralizing phases of rejection attributable only to his hideous appearance; the denial of the love and acceptance he seeks metamorphoses the monster from an innocent creature into a murderous fiend. First, Victor Frankenstein, unwilling to take responsibility for the being to whom he gave life, flees from his monster in mortification and fear for creating not a beautiful new species but instead a horrifying beast. Like his creator, the first villagers the monster encounters do not attempt to communicate with him but immediately shun him in fear of his deformities. Then, the monster spends months learning from and benevolently assisting the virtuous De Lacey family, but despite his best efforts, the family rejects him on sight before he is able to demonstrate his noble intentions. The monster's last hope for acceptance and compassion lies in a female with the same defects as himself, and only Frankenstein possesses the ability to create such a being. In exchange for the monster's promise to live in peace with mankind, Frankenstein agrees to create a female, but the grotesqueness of his work prompts him to tear the body to pieces while the monster looks on. The creature considers this final act of rejection unforgivable; as his last hope of happiness shatters with the rending of the female's body, the monster vows eternal revenge on the man who carelessly gave him life only to withhold the means to enjoy it.

## Works Cited

Shelley, Mary. *Frankenstein*. New York: Bantam, 1991.

## Sample 4: Topic Paper

### Failed Religion

The enfeebled state of religion in America lies at the heart of Melville's <u>Moby Dick</u>. Due in part to their prosperity, the progeny of the austere and steadfast Puritans has lapsed into a state of tolerance and fear. Though the beliefs of their ancestors are still preached from the pulpit, society (as embodied by the crew of the *Pequod*) no longer has the courage to live those beliefs. Aboard the *Pequod* Melville contrasts those without faith to those without strength to those with both but without belief in Christian ideals. While religious toleration sounds peaceful and convenient to social harmony, <u>Moby Dick</u> explores the consequences of a society grown complacent religiously and then confronted with a mortal and spiritual trial. The voyage of the *Pequod* and the fate of its crew represent Melville's expectation for America. Without religious conviction and the strength to defend it, the *Pequod* (and hence America) must ultimately fail the test and suffer the consequent doom.

The strict, Puritan interpretation of Christianity embodied in Father Mapple's sermon failed because of the encroachment of the capitalist society. This interpretation of Christianity demands selflessness in thought and action unknown to the *Pequod*'s crew. In his sermon, Father Mapple says, "...all the things that God would have us do are hard for us to do...and hence, he oftener commands us than endeavors to persuade. And if we obey God, we must disobey ourselves; and it is in this disobeying ourselves, wherein the hardness of obeying God consists" (49). Melville focuses immediately on the difficulty of following God's law, which sets the tone for the decision that Ahab forces Ishmael and Starbuck to make. The ultimate failure of the *Pequod* stems from the inability of the officers and crew to accept the hardship that will follow abandoning the hunt for the white whale, whether that consists of Ahab's outrage at the crew's betrayal or damnation from a higher power at betraying the oath. In his sermon, Mapple continues, noting that "In this world...sin that pays its way can travel freely, and without a passport; whereas Virtue, if a pauper, is stopped at all frontiers" (50). Specifically, Mapple speaks of Jonah, who bought his way aboard a ship bound for Tarshish, but he warns against the allure of wealth that causes men to stray from the righteous path. Whereas virtue and austerity denoted the Puritan lifestyle, the crew of the *Pequod* (and America) concern themselves with the pursuit of wealth that comes of the whale oil. Yet Mapple further reveals the greater difficulty placed upon him: "To preach the Truth to the face of Falsehood!" (53). As a Christian, God calls him to guide those lost to the comforts of the world. Similarly, the Christians aboard the *Pequod* must rectify their situation or face the doom set before them.

In contrast to Father Mapple, Melville creates in Queequeg an individual possessing the aspects of a model Christian—except that he is not Christian. Possessed of devout faith, compassion, and honesty, Queequeg has more in common with the pilgrims of Hawthorne's "The Celestial Railroad" than any other individual in the novel, signifying that the religious conviction that made America strong is now found beyond American borders but not within. Consequently, following his initial, prejudiced impression of Queequeg, Ishmael says, "You cannot hide the soul. Through all his unearthly tattooings, I thought I saw the traces of a simple honest heart..." (55). As compared to Captain Bildad, who sings hymns while trying to cheat Ishmael when the latter formally joins the *Pequod*, Queequeg's simple honesty raises him above the company he keeps. Melville shows the hypocrisy of those who pretend to be Christian. Later, Ishmael notes, "...Queequeg's Ramadan, or Fasting and Humiliation, was to continue all day..." (79). The vigil that the cannibal maintains tests his physical endurance (he foregoes eating and squats without moving for an entire day) as well as his ability to withstand social pressure (Ishmael worries that his friend is dying). The evident self-sacrifice and stoicism bespeak of an individual dedicated to his religion in such a manner as Father Mapple calls his parishioners. In another instance Queequeg alone leaps from the ship and dives after a man who has wrongfully threatened him, saves him, and then, as Ishmael notes, "He did not seem to think that he at all deserved a medal from the Humane and Magnanimous Societies" (64). Queequeg acts justly in accordance with his nature rather than for ulterior motives such as to gain adulation or awards, which are at the root of capitalism in America. In contrast, the Christians aboard the ship watch rather than attempt to aid the drowning man.

Supposedly a good Christian, Ishmael's actions and criticisms of Queequeg betray his lack of religious steadfastness. He lacks both the cannibal's fortitude and conviction. Noting his friend's serene disposition, Ishmael rationalizes, "...what is the will of God?—to do to my fellow man what I would have my fellow man to do to me—that is the will of God" (57). Rather than make himself a model of Christian virtue as Queequeg does with his pagan piety, Ishmael chooses the easier path and joins Queequeg in worshipping Yojo. While Ishmael sees in this the virtue of tolerance, Melville has displayed the flippancy with which a Christian approaches religion. Additionally, Ishmael observes that "...our stiff prejudices grow [elastic] when love once comes to bend them" (58). In his desire to find a friend, Ishmael twists the meaning of God's message instead of trying to teach his friend the virtues of Christianity as Father Mapple intended. His thoughtless acceptance of this behavior exemplifies Melville's concerns regarding religion among his contemporaries. Moreover, when Ishmael finds Queequeg still at his day-long vigil, he says, "...when a man's religion becomes a really frantic; when it is a positive torment to him; and, in fine, makes this earth of ours an uncomfortable inn to lodge in; then I think it high time to take that individual aside and argue the point with him" (82). Ishmael fails to understand the value of the pious cannibal's dedication due to its long absence from his own religious life. When Mapple speaks of the difficulty of obeying God's laws, he means specifically such instances of "torment" that Ishmael tries to dissuade Queequeg from completing.

Yet whereas Ishmael lacks conviction, Starbuck illustrates the tragedy of Christian beliefs when denied the strength to maintain them in the face of adversity. As opposed to his Puritanical predecessors such as John Endicott, Starbuck wilts before the monomaniacal insanity of Captain Ahab. Initially, Starbuck seems prepared to defy Ahab when he demands the oath on the quarterdeck, saying, "To be enraged with a dumb thing, Captain Ahab, seems blasphemous" (139). Only Starbuck says anything against the oath, recalling to Ahab that vengeance belongs only to God, but Ahab manipulates his first mate, subtly reminding the latter of his courage in the hunt and reminding him of the wealth to be gained by the oil of the whale. Thus, more concerned with his reputation and fortune, Starbuck falters. He then concedes, "My soul is more than matched; she's overmanned; and by a madman!" (144). Again, despite the hardness of the trial, Mapple says that Christians should struggle against adversity and Starbuck opts not do so. The spirit of martyrdom does not dwell within him as Melville confronts the relative comfort with which modern Christians have become entrenched. And as the *Pequod*, Melville's abstract microcosm of America, approaches the hour of its test, Melville notes that it is "...morally enfeebled also, by the incompetence of mere unaided virtue or right-mindedness in Starbuck..." (158). The most God-fearing man aboard ship and bearing the responsibility of first mate, Starbuck's duty to himself, the crew, and to God is to confront Ahab before the final lowering against Moby Dick, but he fears to do so, condemning the *Pequod* to failure. Unless religious conviction resurfaces, Melville warns that this fate awaits his weak-willed countrymen.

In stark contrast to his crew, Captain Ahab has the strength of his ancestors and courage of their convictions, yet he has set himself in opposition to Moby Dick and thus leads his crew on a blasphemous mission. If Melville's contention that society must fail if God's laws are not followed is false and Ahab's quest is justified, then the society that will replace will share Ahab's failures. As Melville notes, "...socially, Ahab was inaccessible. Though nominally included in the census of Christendom, he was still an alien to it" (131). Ahab has broken from what Hawthorne called the "magnetic chain of humanity" and thus a society patterned after him must be socially withdrawn, one in which individual concerns outweigh those of humanity. Furthermore, when confronted initially by Starbuck, Ahab preys on his first mate's pride: "From this one poor hunt, then, the best lance out of all Nantucket, surely he will not hang back, when every foremast-hand has clutched a whetstone? Ah! Constrainings seize thee; I see!" (140). An America that preys on the individual must ultimately devour itself from within as Ahab's manipulations bring about Starbuck's eventual demise. But Ahab recognizes his folly. He says to Starbuck, "...let me look into a human eye; it is better than to gaze into sea or sky; better than to gaze upon God. By the green land; by the bright hearth-stone! This is the magic glass, man; I see my wife and my child in then eye" (406). Starbuck reminds Ahab of his need for human connection. Thus Ahab knows that his manipulations and seclusion are in error and deny him an attainable felicity. Melville recognizes that such a society must fail, for it has no purpose in continuing.

The resolution of <u>Moby Dick</u> reveals the folly of an American society lacking the religious demeanor of its founders. Unless the preaching of Father Mapple takes root in vacuous Ishmael, the latter will put to sea again and again without hope of finding lasting peace. In contrast, Melville's portrayal of Queequeg as a noble savage focuses on that which Ishmael admires, but his strength cannot save him without a meaningful purpose to direct it against the manipulations of a trial such as Ahab. Similarly, Starbuck's religious purpose lacks the strength to contend with the hardship of which Father Mapple warns. Ahab works destructively in opposition to both Queequeg's strength and Starbuck's purpose, manipulating those such as Ishmael to blunt any attack that Starbuck could make. Without strength working in tandem with moral purpose, the *Pequod* (and America) must sink at the last.

Works Cited

Melville, Herman. <u>Moby Dick</u>. New York: Norton, 2002 (1851).

# How to Identify Valid Secondary Sources

# How to Identify Valid Secondary Sources

## Criteria for a Valid Secondary Source

1. The article must be an objective analysis of the topic; subjective, editorial or anecdotal commentary is not valid.

2. Full text articles only. Do not use abstracts, summaries and dictionary or encyclopedia references.

3. All articles should have an author; furthermore, the author should be an expert in his/her field of study. If the author is not listed, you must research the origin of the author and defend his/her validity.

4. The article should have a bibliography or works cited to indicate research. If the article does not document any outside sources, you must research the origin of the author and defend his/her validity.

5. If there is any question about the credibility of the article, you must ask the instructor to validate it.

# Annotated Bibliography

# Annotated Bibliography

## Definition:

- The Annotated Bibliography is the sixth stage in the composition process.

- This stage combines objective research from a Secondary Source with information from your Topic and Subtopics.

- The Annotated Bibliography should be used to create viable Body Paragraphs for the Rough Draft and Final Draft.

## Requirements:

- The following sample provides the exact requirements for each section of the Annotated Bibliography.

- Pay particular attention to the words in **bold type**.

- Remember to use objective language, a variety of sentence styles, appropriate transitions, and proper parenthetical citations.

- Remember to provide a photocopy of the secondary source. You must also highlight the information you will provide in the Annotated Bibliography.

- Use the Topic Paper for information on the Primary Source.

- Use the highlighted photocopy of the Secondary Source.

# Sample Annotated Bibliography

Last Name 1

Full Name

Instructor

Class

Day Month Year

Working Title for the Paper

**Insert the bibliographic reference from the secondary source after your working title.**

*Note: You must consult the MLA handbook to correctly format the reference for your source.*

**Direct Evidence from the Secondary Source**—This passage establishes the exact information that you will use from the secondary source. This secondary information will also be used in the body paragraphs of your paper. (Page number)

*Note: This passage is justified, single-spaced and indented 1-inch from the 1-inch margin of the paper. Limit each passage to 10 sentences.*

**Remember:**

Begin Analysis Paragraph on page 2 of the Annotated Bibliography

1.  Provide a Subtopic sentence.

2.  Provide a sentence to limit and define the Subtopic sentence.

3.  Introduce Primary evidence as well as its important concept. [Note: use the necessary punctuation or method to introduce the quote.]

4.  Provide direct, paraphrased or summarized evidence from the Primary Source. [Consult your instructor on which method to use for the assignment.]

5.  Analyze Primary source information as it relates to the topic and the Thesis Statement or point you wish to prove.

3.  Introduce Secondary evidence as well as its important concept. [Note: use the necessary punctuation or method to introduce the quote.]

4.  Provide direct, paraphrased or summarized evidence from the Secondary Source. [Consult your instructor on which method to use for the assignment.]

5.  Analyze Secondary Source information as it relates to the topic and the Thesis Statement or point you wish to prove.

3.  Introduce Primary evidence as well as its important concept. [Note: use the necessary punctuation or method to introduce the quote.]

4.  Provide direct, paraphrased or summarized evidence from the Primary Source. [Consult your instructor on which method to use for the assignment.]

5.  Analyze Primary Source information as it relates to the topic and the Thesis Statement or point you wish to prove.

3.  Introduce Secondary evidence as well as its important concept. [Note: use the necessary punctuation or method to introduce the quote.]

4. **Provide direct, paraphrased or summarized evidence from the Secondary source.** [Consult your instructor on which method to use for the assignment.]

5. **Analyze Secondary Source information as it relates to the topic and the Thesis Statement or point you wish to prove.**

3. **Introduce Primary evidence as well as its important concept.** [Note: use the necessary punctuation or method to introduce the quote.]

4. **Provide direct, paraphrased or summarized evidence from the source.** [Consult your instructor on which method to use for the assignment.]

5. **Analyze Primary Source information as it relates to the topic and the Thesis Statement or point you wish to prove and transition into the next paragraph.**

# Student
# Samples

# Sample 1: Annotated Bibliography

Transitional Giotto Paragraph 1

Eimerl, Sarel. The World of Giotto. Alexandria, Virginia: Time-Life Books, 1967.

Instead of using glittering gold background which previous painters had employed to create and aura of supernatural mystery, he placed his figures in settings of hills, meadows and houses familiar to any Italian (9).

Whereas previous painters had disposed their figures with little regard for their relationships, he arranged people in a meaningful, natural manner (9).

Painting in the Medieval Period, like most art before the Renaissance enlightenment, is not created for the common man; thus most of these old paintings are not easy identifiable to true human life, mainly because of their unrealistic appearance. The lack of realism spawns from the artists' use of flat patterns in large areas, managing compositional devices poorly, and the under-abundance of naturalist ideas. In response to viewing the new realistic style of Giotto, James Snyder declares, "Gone are the gold lines that are usually shot through the costumes and the crisp linear patterns for the draperies" (460). The patterns artists use to adorn the borders and garments in their paintings create a deceptive perspective that hinders the feasibility and practicality of the paintings; Giotto abandons this technique to create three-dimensionality in his works. Similarly, Sarel Eimerl in *The World of Giotto* demonstrates how medieval painters use the gold for other reasons, as well, "Instead of using glittering gold background which previous painters had employed to create and aura of supernatural mystery, he [Giotto] placed his figures in settings of hills, meadows and houses familiar to any Italian" (9). While the gold adds an air of regality, it also makes the painting appear flat, the very concept that Giotto strives to dispose of. Compositional devices often enhance a work of art; however, in the Medieval Period, compositional devices impede the plausibility of the subject as an appropriate depiction of the truth: "Giotto avoids such obvious compositional devices as symmetry and centrality" (Snyder 463). While compositional devices often direct the viewer to the desired subject, such noticeable methods often manipulate and misplace the subject beyond the reach of logical arrangement. On the contrary, some painters in the past do not concern themselves with the placement of the figures and focus only on the execution of the figures themselves: "Whereas previous painters had disposed their figures with little regard for their relationships, he arranged people in a meaningful, natural manner" (Eimerl 9). Using logic can prove that randomly placed figures in a work of art create chaos and an unnatural composition, developing scenes consisting of imaginary people and relationships among them. New ideas arise during Giotto's lifetime that influence the change in style representative of his paintings; for example, "the naturalism of his paintings echoes the sentiments expressed by Saint Francis of Assisi, who made religion a simple, everyday experience that was emotionally appealing to the common man" (Snyder 460). Naturalism is the essential idea that Giotto strives to establish in his paintings so that art, like religion, can relate to and interest the common man.

## Sample 2: Annotated Bibliography

Objection to Rejection

Brooks, Peter. "'Godlike Science/Unhallowed Arts': Language, Nature, and Monstrosity." *Mary Shelley*. Ed. Harold Bloom. Modern Critical Views. New York: Chelsea, 1985.

> Mutual sympathy, benefaction, protection, and relation are close to being sealed through language, when Felix, Agatha, and Safie enter and throw the situation brutally back into the speculary order: Agatha faints, Safie flees, and Felix "tore me from his father, to whose knees I clung." The result is Fall. The Monster becomes explicitly satanic—"I, like the arch-fiend, bore a hell within me," sets fire to the De Laceys' abandoned cottage, and sets forth into the world in search of his creator, the *deus absconditus* who alone now can restore, through a second creation, the Monster to the chain of living sympathies. (106)

Nelson, Lowry, Jr. "Night Thoughts on the Gothic Novel." *Mary Shelley*. Ed. Harold Bloom. Modern Critical Views. New York: Chelsea, 1985.

> The family in horror flee the house forever, and the monster burns it in a wild fury. He has undeservedly fallen from grace and he himself destroys his former Eden. (39).

> But Frankenstein cannot bring himself to perform such a second horror of creation. (40)

Despite his devastating first encounter with civilization, the monster's nature remains gentle and he performs gracious deeds for the De Lacey family for months; when he reveals his presence, however, the De Laceys reject him on sight. The blind De Lacey, whom the monster seeks first, recognizes his gentleness, but the other family members, influenced by sight, perceive him as dangerous and attack him before he can demonstrate his noble nature. Scarred from his previous treatment by humans, the monster refrains from immediately presenting himself to the De Laceys and spends time studying their behavior; during this time he discovers the reason for his previous rejection and the importance of verbal communication:

> I had admired the perfect forms of my cottagers...but how was I terrified when I viewed myself in a transparent pool! At first I started back, unable to believe that it was indeed I who was reflected in the mirror; and when I became fully convinced that I was in reality the monster that I am, I was filled with the bitterest sensations of despondence and mortification....I formed in my imagination a thousand pictures of presenting myself to them, and their reception of me. I imagined that they would be disgusted, until, by my gentle demeanour and conciliating words, I should first win their favour and afterwards their love. (Shelley 98-100)

Fully aware of his unnatural physical deformity and the effect it has on humans, the monster decides to first entreat the friendship to the blind father, who will then be able to act as a mediator between him and the rest of the family; however, the creature's plan takes an unfortunate turn as the young De Laceys return in the midst of their first meeting. In his critical essay entitled "'Godlike Science/Unhallowed Arts': Language, Nature, and Monstrosity," Peter Brooks describes the scene in which the young De Laceys enter the cottage and discover the monster conversing with their father: "Mutual sympathy, benefaction, protection, and relation are close to being sealed through language, when Felix, Agatha, and Safie enter and throw the situation brutally back into the speculary order: Agatha faints, Safie flees," and Felix furiously tears the monster from his father's knees and beats him (106). Sight overpowers language as the De Laceys assume the creature sitting by the father is dangerous simply because he appears that way; they do not wait for an explanation from either their father or the monster before acting. The monster's dream of acceptance shatters when the family he has loved and assisted unseen for many months rejects him on sight. In response, he swears revenge against mankind, but later "when I considered what had passed at the cottage, I could not help believing that I had been too hasty in my conclusions. It was apparent my conversation had interested the father in my behalf, and I was a fool in having exposed my person to the horror of his children...I resolved to return to the cottage, seek the old man, and by my representations win him to my party" (Shelley 122). The creature accepts blame for his violent eviction from the cottage in hope of a second chance to convey his desire for friendship and compassion. However, as Lowry Nelson, Jr. relates in his critical essay "Night Thoughts on the Gothic Novel," the monster returns to the cottage only to find it abandoned: "The family in horror flee the house forever, and the monster burns it in a wild fury. He has undeservedly fallen from grace and he himself destroys his former Eden" (39). The De Laceys' merciless treatment of the monster justifies the creature's fury; they, as well as anyone who rejects him simply in response to his physical appearance, are responsible for the creature's transformation from one who seeks friendship to one who seeks revenge. The monster describes the devastating effect of this one act of rejection on his once loving nature: "For the first time the feelings of revenge and hatred filled my bosom, and I did not strive to control them, but...I bent my mind towards injury and death" (Shelley 123). The creature is willing and able to endure the hatred and scorn of strangers, but the condemnation of a family he loves and generously serves casts on his disposition an indelible shadow of hatred.

# Rough Draft

# Rough Draft

## Definition:

- The Rough Draft is the seventh stage in the composition process and is a synthesis of the Topic Paper and Annotated Bibliographies. This stage also provides an objective, researched analysis of the Primary and Secondary Sources.

## Requirements:

- The following outline provides the exact requirements for each section of the Rough Draft.

- Pay particular attention to the words in **bold type**.

- Remember to use objective language, a variety of sentence styles, appropriate transitions, and proper parenthetical citations.

- Use the Topic Paper for information on the Primary Source.

- Use the highlighted photocopy of the Secondary Source.

- Use the Annotated Bibliography to create viable Body Paragraphs for the Rough Draft.

# Sample Rough Draft

Full Name

Instructor

Class

Day Month Year

Title for the Paper

**Thesis Paragraph**: This introductory paragraph of your paper should explore the following questions: **Note—*Do not* type the questions.**

**WHAT** is the topic?

❖ Establish the author title and General Topic of the Primary Source and paper.

❖ Provide a transition sentence to define and limit the General Topic.

**HOW** will the topic be proven?

❖ Establish the **first Subtopic** and its general connection to the main topic.

❖ Establish the **second Subtopic** and its general connection to the main topic.

❖ Establish the **third Subtopic** and its general connection to the main topic.

• *Remember these Subtopics will be the basis for the topic sentences in the Body Paragraphs of your paper, so create **key phrases** that* *will help identify the Subtopics when you produce these Body Paragraphs.*

<u>**WHY** is this topic important?</u>

❖ The last sentence of the thesis paragraph is called the Thesis Statement; this statement is the point you will prove in the paper and provides the logical conclusion given the General Topic and Subtopics.

<u>**First Body Paragraph**</u>:

1. **Provide a Subtopic sentence.**

2. **Provide a sentence to limit and define the Subtopic sentence.**

3. **Introduce Primary evidence as well as its important concept.** [Note: use the necessary punctuation or method to introduce the quote.]

4. **Provide direct, paraphrased or summarized evidence from the Primary Source.** [Consult your instructor on which method to use for the assignment.]

5. **Analyze Primary source information as it relates to the topic and the Thesis Statement or point you wish to prove.**

3. **Introduce Secondary evidence as well as its important concept.** [Note: use the necessary punctuation or method to introduce the quote.]

4. **Provide direct, paraphrased or summarized evidence from the Secondary source.** [Consult your instructor on which method to use for the assignment.]

5. **Analyze Secondary Source information as it relates to the topic and the Thesis Statement or point you wish to prove.**

3.  Introduce Primary evidence as well as its important concept. [Note: use the necessary punctuation or method to introduce the quote.]

4.  Provide direct, paraphrased or summarized evidence from the source. [Consult your instructor on which method to use for the assignment.]

5.  Analyze Primary Source information as it relates to the topic and the Thesis Statement or point you wish to prove.

3.  Introduce Secondary evidence as well as its important concept. [Note: use the necessary punctuation or method to introduce the quote.]

4.  Provide direct, paraphrased or summarized evidence from the Secondary Source. [Consult your instructor on which method to use for the assignment.]

5.  Analyze Secondary Source information as it relates to the topic and the Thesis Statement or point you wish to prove.

3.  Introduce Primary evidence as well as its important concept. [Note: use the necessary punctuation or method to introduce the quote.]

4.  Provide direct, paraphrased or summarized evidence from the source. [Consult your instructor on which method to use for the assignment.]

5.  Analyze Primary Source information as it relates to the topic and the Thesis Statement or point you wish to prove and transition into the next paragraph.

<u>Second Body Paragraph</u>:

1.  Provide a Subtopic sentence.

2.  Provide a sentence to limit and define the Subtopic sentence.

3.  Introduce Primary evidence as well as its important concept. [Note: use the necessary punctuation or method to introduce the quote.]

4.  Provide direct, paraphrased or summarized evidence from the Primary Source. [Consult your instructor on which method to use for the assignment.]

5.  Analyze Primary Source information as it relates to the topic and the Thesis Statement or point you wish to prove.

3.  Introduce Secondary evidence as well as its important concept. [Note: use the necessary punctuation or method to introduce the quote.]

4.  Provide direct, paraphrased or summarized evidence from the Secondary Source. [Consult your instructor on which method to use for the assignment.]

5.  Analyze Secondary Source information as it relates to the topic and the Thesis Statement or point you wish to prove.

3.  Introduce Primary evidence as well as its important concept. [Note: use the necessary punctuation or method to introduce the quote.]

4.  Provide direct, paraphrased or summarized evidence from the source. [Consult your instructor on which method to use for the assignment.]

5.  Analyze Primary Source information as it relates to the topic and the Thesis Statement or point you wish to prove.

3.  Introduce Secondary evidence as well as its important concept. [Note: use the necessary punctuation or method to introduce the quote.]

4. Provide direct, paraphrased or summarized evidence from the Secondary Source. [Consult your instructor on which method to use for the assignment.]

5. Analyze Secondary Source information as it relates to the topic and the Thesis Statement or point you wish to prove.

3. Introduce Primary evidence as well as its important concept. [Note: use the necessary punctuation or method to introduce the quote.]

4. Provide direct, paraphrased or summarized evidence from the source. [Consult your instructor on which method to use for the assignment.]

5. Analyze Primary Source information as it relates to the topic and the Thesis Statement or point you wish to prove and transition into the next paragraph.

Third Body Paragraph:

1. Provide a Subtopic sentence.

2. Provide a sentence to limit and define the Subtopic sentence.

3. Introduce Primary evidence as well as its important concept. [Note: use the necessary punctuation or method to introduce the quote.]

4. Provide direct, paraphrased or summarized evidence from the source. [Consult your instructor on which method to use for the assignment.]

5. Analyze Primary Source information as it relates to the topic and the Thesis Statement or point you wish to prove.

3. Introduce Secondary evidence as well as its important concept. [Note: use the necessary punctuation or method to introduce the quote.]

4.   Provide direct, paraphrased or summarized evidence from the Secondary Source. [Consult your instructor on which method to use for the assignment.]

5.   Analyze Secondary Source information as it relates to the topic and the Thesis Statement or point you wish to prove.

3.   Introduce Primary evidence as well as its important concept. [Note: use the necessary punctuation or method to introduce the quote.]

4.   Provide direct, paraphrased or summarized evidence from the source. [Consult your instructor on which method to use for the assignment.

5.   Analyze Primary Source information as it relates to the topic and the Thesis Statement or point you wish to prove.

3.   Introduce Secondary evidence as well as its important concept. [Note: use the necessary punctuation or method to introduce the quote.]

4.   Provide direct, paraphrased or summarized evidence from the Secondary Source. [Consult your instructor on which method to use for the assignment.]

5.   Analyze Secondary Source information as it relates to the topic and the Thesis Statement or point you wish to prove.

3.   Introduce Primary evidence as well as its important concept. [Note: use the necessary punctuation or method to introduce the quote.]

4.   Provide direct, paraphrased or summarized evidence from the source. [Consult your instructor on which method to use for the assignment.]

5. Analyze Primary Source information as it relates to the topic and the Thesis Statement or point you wish to prove and transition into the conclusion.

## Conclusion

❖ Reassert the **Thesis Statement** of the paper.

❖ Review the strongest supporting examples from the **Thesis Paragraph** of the paper.

❖ **Do not** introduce anything new in the conclusion.

## Works Cited

Insert the bibliographic reference from the Primary and Secondary Sources in alphabetical order.

*Note: You must consult the MLA handbook to correctly format the reference for your source.*

Student Sample

# Sample 1: Rough Draft

## Transitional Giotto

James Snyder's *Medieval Art* recalls the famous Italian artist, Giotto di Bondone, bringing the Medieval Period to a close by developing new concepts for the fresco style of painting, thus establishing a basis for the prominent painters of the Renaissance Period. Giotto combines old ideas with new techniques, consequently creating a style more characteristic of legendary Renaissance painters. Italian paintings in the old Greek and Byzantine styles before and during Giotto's lifetime consist of flat, two-dimensional figures. Giotto brings about a more realistic style of painting that discards several old ways of painting and thinking in an effort to construct a new way of creating and viewing paintings. As a transitional artist between the Middle Ages and the Renaissance, Giotto influences the painters of the European Renaissance Period through his change of style, thus making Giotto's style apparent in future artists' works. Before, during, and after the Medieval Period, art is progressively becoming more realistic and understandable to the common man; Giotto is one of many painters to take a big step towards changing the style successfully while retaining the inherent dignity that forever remains with prestigious painting.

Painting in the Medieval Period, like most art before the Renaissance enlightenment, is not created for the common man; thus most of these old paintings are not easy identifiable to true human life, mainly because of their unrealistic appearance. The lack of realism spawns from the artists' use of flat patterns in large areas, managing compositional devices poorly, and the under-abundance of naturalist ideas. In response to viewing the new realistic style of Giotto, James Snyder declares, "Gone are the gold lines that are usually shot through the costumes and the crisp linear patterns for the draperies" (460). The patterns artists use to adorn the borders and garments in their paintings create a deceptive perspective that hinders the feasibility and practicality of the paintings; Giotto abandons this technique to create three-dimensionality in his works. Medieval painters use the gold for other reasons, as well, "Instead of using glittering gold background which previous painters had employed to create and aura of supernatural mystery, he [Giotto] placed his figures in settings of hills, meadows and houses familiar to any Italian" (Eimerl 9). While the gold adds an air of regality, it also makes the painting appear flat, the very concept that Giotto strives to dispose of. Compositional devices often enhance a work of art; however, in the Medieval Period, compositional devices impede the plausibility of the subject as an appropriate depiction of the truth: "Giotto avoids such obvious compositional devices as symmetry and centrality" (Snyder 463). While compositional devices often direct the viewer to the desired subject, such noticeable methods often manipulate and misplace the subject beyond the reach of logical arrangement. On the contrary, some painters in the past do not concern themselves with the placement of the figures and focus only on the execution of the figures themselves; Eimerl confirms this, saying, "Whereas previous painters had disposed their figures with little regard for their relationships, he arranged people in a meaningful, natural manner" (9). Using logic can prove that randomly placed figures in a work of art create chaos and an unnatural composition, developing scenes consisting of imaginary people and relationships among them. New ideas arise during Giotto's lifetime that influence the change in style representative of his paintings; for example, "the naturalism of his paintings echoes the sentiments expressed by Saint Francis of Assisi, who made religion a simple, everyday experience that was emotionally appealing to the common man" (Snyder 460). Naturalism is the essential idea that Giotto strives to establish in his paintings so that art, like religion, can relate to and interest the common man.

In a quest to portray the subjects exactly as they are in reality, Giotto develops a new style of painting that incorporates both old and new ideas and techniques. To achieve realism, Giotto uses depth and perspective, recognizable human emotions, and figures' body language and posture. The first step in creating a believable atmosphere is to create proper perspective; Mr. Snyder states that Giotto institutes "a new sense of space [...in which] the three-dimensional qualities of the figures are powerfully stated [...] evoking the qualities of objects we wish to touch as large rounded volumes, as if they were sculptures and no longer flat patterns" (460). The composition is becoming a real world in which a sense of space forms a reasonable scene that people perceive as an accurate depiction of reality. James Barter presents an example of this perspective and special depth in Giotto's representation of a castle in a Biblical painting: "Rather than rendering the castle as a flat two-dimensional figure, Giotto gives it three-dimensional depth that the viewer sees at the corners; the walls in the foreground appear closer to the viewer than do those in the background" (25). Although this concept merely applies to common sense, previous artists overlook the need to create a realistic painting that possesses the same special depth as the real world.

Once Giotto establishes the atmosphere, he paints people in an innovative style; "Human emotions are now registered; a new warmth and intimacy are projected. Real people are placed before our eyes" (Snyder 460). The work of art is now becoming more personal with subjects that experience everyday issues and have feelings; thus breaking away from the standard mug shot pose for portraits and biblical scenes. The eminent modern artist Henri Matisse writes, "'When I see Giotto's frescos at Padua I do not trouble to find out which scene of the life of Christ is before me, for I understand at once the feeling which radiates from it [...]'" (Eimerl 8). For the average person, much less an pre-Expressionist painter, understanding the exact emotion and meaning the artist conveys in the work is often difficult in a realistic painting; therefore, Giotto's skillful style of creating recognizable, human figures is revolutionary for his time and for modern times. In contrast to the recognizable compositional devises of earlier times to appropriately direct the viewer's attention, Mr. Snyder affirms, "Giotto controls our attention span through the subtle psychology of directional focus of all figures [...with the] figures closing the compositional field" (464). The more natural flow to specific points of focus in Giotto's paintings makes for a more peaceful composition that is more pleasing to look at than previous works of art that lack appropriate harmony.

Giotto's revolutionary painting techniques became some of the recognizable characteristics of the European Renaissance that follows shortly after his death. Proof of Giotto's influence lies in the first famous Italian Renaissance artist, the Sistine Chapel masterpiece, and the concepts of various legendary artists' of the Renaissance. Although Giotto is not technically is not a part of the Renaissance period, Snyder titles him "the precursor of Masaccio, the first great Renaissance painter in Florence" (460). The innovative style and ideas of Giotto immediately influence artists in Italy, such as Masaccio, which spawns the beginning of a new era in artistic endeavors. The Economist online magazine confirms the relationship between Masaccio and Giotto, "[...] his style was far more naturalistic than that of his predecessors and his psychological depiction was rivaled only by Giotto" (1). Since Masaccio is the first great Renaissance painter, Giotto becomes a great influence for all artists of many centuries after his death because of his technique and innovations in the way to involve the viewer in art. Giotto receives a commission to paint the interior of a chapel "with a vaulted ceiling [...with] Giotto's task to articulate the barren into an elaborate gallery [...] and he divided the side walls [...to paint] a sequence of narratives" (Snyder 460,462).

The pictorial Bible narratives Giotto paints in his chapel job are the foundation for the Sistine Chapel that Michelangelo paints centuries later; even the procedure by which Giotto divides areas into block sections resembles the layout of the later chapel. Regarding the famous chapel Giotto is commission to adorn with glorious paintings, Barter states, "All artists have their magnum opus—the one masterpiece that expresses their genius above all others. For Giotto, the great work was the Arena Chapel" (23). When someone mentions the painter Michelangelo, most people think of the magnificent Sistine Chapel paintings; similarly, people associate the Arena Chapel paintings with Giotto as his greatest feat of works. Numerous other artists born after the Middle Ages appreciate the transformation by Giotto: "He was praised by Dante as a leader in the arts," and "Vasari named him the first truly 'modern' artist to break from the 'crude manner of the Greeks'" (Snyder 460). Artists' and writers praise Giotto for the innovations he makes in painting to make painting more reasonable, which is necessary in a time when scientific theories and advancements are becoming more popular.

Before, during, and after the Medieval Period, art is progressively becoming more realistic and understandable to the common man; Giotto is one of many painters to take a big step towards changing the style successfully while retaining the inherent dignity that forever remains with prestigious painting. Creating new ideas with old techniques and subjects, Giotto creates an innovative style that is more realistic than that of previous paintings. He paves the way for Renaissance artists, which is noticeable in comparing his work with that of famous Renaissance painters; thus making him a legendary transitional artist.

## Works Cited

Barter, James. <u>Artists of the Renaissance</u>. San Diego: Lucent Books, 1999.

Eimerl, Sarel. <u>The World of Giotto.</u> Alexandria, Virginia: Time-Life Books, 1967.

"Masaccio's Panels." <u>The Economist</u> 22 September 2001. 27 September 2003 <http://infotrac-college.thomsonlearning.com/itw/infomark/935/63/64956808w3/10!ar fmt>.

Snyder, James. <u>Medieval Art</u>. Harry N. Abrams, Inc.: New York, 1989.

# Final Draft

# Final Draft

## Definition:

- The Final Draft is the eighth stage in the composition process and provides a stylistically flawless, objective, researched analysis of the Primary and Secondary Sources.

- The Final Draft is an edited and revised copy of the Rough Draft.

- Since the Rough Draft and Final Draft contain the same structure, just use the model for the Rough Draft shown in the *Tao of Composition*. **Remember to revise the Rough Draft according to the changes made during the editing process.**

## Requirements:

- Edited copy of the Rough Draft

- Remember to use objective language, a variety of sentence styles, appropriate transitions, and proper parenthetical citations.

# Student
# Samples

# Sample 1: Final Draft

## Objection to Rejection

In her Gothic novel *Frankenstein*, Mary Shelley portrays Victor Frankenstein's monster as an innocent creature who, as a result of paternal and societal rejection, metamorphoses into a murderous fiend. The rejection the monster suffers originates from an innate fear of the hideous; humans who look upon his repulsive countenance react in fear and disgust. During the creature's first interactions with humanity, the man who forms him and the inhabitants of the village into which he wanders act instinctively on their fears instead of attempting to communicate with the monster in an effort to learn his desires and intentions. Despite his devastating first encounters with civilization, the monster's nature remains gentle and he performs gracious deeds for the De Lacey family for months before exposing his presence. He first seeks the blind De Lacey, who recognizes his gentleness, but the other family members, influenced by sight, assume he is dangerous and attack before he is able to reveal his noble nature. The monster's last hope for acceptance and contentment lies in a female with the same defects as himself, whom only Frankenstein has the ability to create. Frankenstein agrees to create a female, but the hideousness of his work causes him to tear the body to pieces before the monster's eyes in a final, unforgivable, act of rejection. The monster experiences three progressively devastating levels of rejection based on physical appearance; the denial of the love and acceptance he seeks transforms the monster from an innocent creation into a bitter fiend who vows revenge against mankind.

Despite the creature's innocent intentions in his first interactions with civilization, humans who behold his frightening countenance react in fright and horror. The inhabitants of the first village into which he wanders, as well as the man who forms him, know nothing of the creature's intentions or desires; they act on instinctive fear of the deformed appearance without attempting to communicate with the monster. Instead of triumph, Victor Frankenstein's reaction is one of shock as he accomplishes his aspiration to create life from dead material:

> His limbs were in proportion, and I had selected his features as beautiful. Beautiful! Great God! His yellow skin scarcely covered the work of muscles and arteries beneath; his hair was of a lustrous black, and flowing; his teeth of a pearly

whiteness; but these luxuriances only formed a more horrid contrast with his watery eyes, that seemed almost of the same colour as the dun-white sockets in which they were set, his shriveled complexion and straight black lips. (Shelley 42)

Before his moment of achievement, Frankenstein's obsession with his project blinds him to its consequences, but now he can no longer deny the outcome of his actions: his creation is not an accomplishment to be proclaimed but a monstrosity to be feared. In his introduction to the book *Mary Shelley*, from the Modern Critical Views series, Harold Bloom describes the effect that the realization of his dream has on Frankenstein: "When the 'dull yellow eye' of his creature opens, this creator falls from the autonomy of a supreme artificer to the terror of a child of earth...He flees his responsibility..." (6). Instead of scientific renown, Frankenstein now desires escape from his hideous creation; without attempting to communicate with the monster, he denies his parental responsibilities and flees. Frankenstein flees not in fear of injury, for the monster makes no aggressive moves; his fear stems from the creature's deformity: "No mortal could support the horror of that countenance. A mummy again endued with animation could not be so hideous as that wretch. I had gazed on him while unfinished; he was ugly then, but when those muscles and joints were rendered capable of motion, it became a thing such as even Dante could not have conceived" (Shelley 43). Before animating the creature, Frankenstein cannot foresee the effect that life will have on an already unsightly form; the result of animation is a living monster whose form is horrible beyond his creator's imagination. Unwilling to take responsibility for his mistake, Frankenstein abandons his creature, which "either would not have happened or would not have mattered anyway, if Frankenstein had been an aesthetically successful maker; a beautiful 'monster,' or even a passable one, would not have been a monster" (Bloom 5). Frankenstein would desire recognition for the creation of a beautiful being, and a society prejudiced against the hideous would welcome an attractive creature. However, the creature is not beautiful, and society immediately rejects him: "I [the monster] had hardly set my foot within the door before the children shrieked, and one of the women fainted. The whole village was roused; some fled, some attacked me, until, grievously bruised by stones and many other kinds of missile weapons, I escaped to the open country...miserable...from the barbarity of man" (Shelley 91).

The monster enters the village innocently seeking nourishment, but the villagers, due to his horrifying countenance, assume he is dangerous and attack without attempting to discover his intentions.

Despite his devastating first encounter with civilization, the monster's nature remains gentle and he performs gracious deeds for the De Lacey family for months; when he reveals his presence, however, the De Laceys reject him on sight. The blind De Lacey, whom the monster seeks first, recognizes his gentleness, but the other family members, influenced by sight, perceive him as dangerous and attack him before he can demonstrate his noble nature. Scarred from his previous treatment by humans, the monster refrains from immediately presenting himself to the De Laceys and spends time studying their behavior; during this time he discovers the reason for his previous rejection and the importance of verbal communication:

> I had admired the perfect forms of my cottagers...but how was I terrified when I viewed myself in a transparent pool! At first I started back, unable to believe that it was indeed I who was reflected in the mirror; and when I became fully convinced that I was in reality the monster that I am, I was filled with the bitterest sensations of despondence and mortification...I formed in my imagination a thousand pictures of presenting myself to them, and their reception of me. I imagined that they would be disgusted, until, by my gentle demeanour and conciliating words, I should first win their favour and afterwards their love. (Shelley 98-100)

Fully aware of his unnatural physical deformity and the effect it has on humans, the monster decides to first entreat the friendship to the blind father, who will then be able to act as a mediator between him and the rest of the family; however, the creature's plan takes an unfortunate turn as the young De Laceys return in the midst of their first meeting. In his critical essay entitled "'Godlike Science/Unhallowed Arts': Language, Nature, and Monstrosity," Peter Brooks describes the scene in which the young De Laceys enter the cottage and discover the monster conversing with their father: "Mutual sympathy, benefaction, protection, and relation are close to being sealed through language, when Felix, Agatha, and Safie enter and throw the situation brutally back into the speculary order: Agatha faints, Safie flees," and Felix furiously tears the monster from his father's knees and beats him (106). Sight overpowers language as the De Laceys assume the creature sitting by the father is dangerous simply because he appears that way; they do not wait for an explanation from either their father or the monster before acting. The monster's dream of acceptance shatters when the family he has loved and assisted unseen for many months rejects him on sight. In response, he swears revenge against mankind, but later "when I considered what had passed at the cottage, I could not help believing that I had been too hasty in my conclusions...It was apparent my conversation had interested the father in my behalf, and I was a fool in having exposed my person to the horror of his children...I resolved to return to the cottage, seek the old man, and by my representations win him to my party" (Shelley 122). The creature accepts blame for his violent eviction from the cottage in hope of a second chance to convey his desire for friendship and compassion. However, as Lowry Nelson, Jr. relates in his critical essay "Night Thoughts on the Gothic Novel," the monster returns to the cottage only to find it abandoned: "The family in horror flee the house forever, and the monster burns it in a wild fury. He has undeservedly fallen from grace and he himself destroys his former Eden" (39). The De Laceys' merciless treatment of the monster justifies the creature's fury; they, as well as anyone who rejects him simply in response to his physical appearance, are responsible for the creature's transformation from one who seeks friendship to one who seeks revenge. The monster describes the devastating effect of this one act of rejection on his once loving nature: "For the first time the feelings of revenge and hatred filled my bosom, and I did not strive to control them, but...I bent my mind towards injury and death" (Shelley 123). The creature is willing and able to endure the hatred and scorn of strangers, but the condemnation of a family he loves and generously serves casts on his disposition an indelible shadow of hatred.

After coming to know the monster through the creature's personal testimony, Frankenstein agrees to create a female; however, the hideousness of his work causes him to tear the body to pieces before the monster's eyes in a final act of rejection. The creature vows to act in peace towards humanity if Frankenstein will make him happy; the promise and then denial of his single request provokes the monster to revenge. While conversing with his creator, the monster describes the agony of living in a world whose inhabitants are unable to accept a creature with his hideous and misshapen form: "Let him [man] live with me in the interchange of kindness, and instead of injury I would bestow every benefit upon him with tears of gratitude at his acceptance. But that cannot be; the human senses are insurmountable barriers to our union" (Shelley 130). The monster abandons all hope of acceptance and friendship from any member of the human race, for he deems the union of human sight and his own repulsiveness impossible. One chance of happiness remains for the monster; after he burns the De Laceys cottage, he "sets forth into the world in search of his creator...who alone can restore, through a second creation, the Monster to the chain of living sympathies" (Brooks 106). When he makes contact with Frankenstein, the monster implores him to commence the creation of a female, for his only hope of acceptance lies in another being with the same defects as himself. Even as he entreats Frankenstein's compassion through his personal testimony, however, his hideous form prevents his creator's sympathy: "I [Frankenstein] compassionated him and sometimes felt a wish to console him, but when I looked upon him, when I saw the filthy mass that moved and talked, my heart sickened and my feelings were altered to those of horror and hatred" (Shelley 132). After hearing his creature's life story, Frankenstein now understands his thoughts, feelings, and desires; however, like at the time of creation, Frankenstein's failure to love results from the monster's physical gruesomeness. The monster's constant pleas eventually lead Frankenstein to take partial responsibility for his creature's happiness, and he agrees to create the female; however, when he begins his work, "Frankenstein cannot bring himself to perform such a second horror of creation" (Nelson 40). Frankenstein allows the physical repulsion he feels as he beholds the female's unfinished form to take precedence over his responsibility for the monster's happiness and his responsibility to protect his family and friends from the monster's wrath. In a final act of rejection, Frankenstein denies his creature's last hope for happiness and "tore to pieces the thing on which I was engaged. The wretch saw me destroy the creature on whose future existence he depended for happiness, and with a howl of devilish despair and revenge, withdrew" (Shelley 151). As Frankenstein destroys his last dream of companionship, the monster vows revenge on the man who carelessly created life and then denied his creature the means to enjoy it.

Frankenstein's monster endures three progressively demoralizing phases of rejection attributable only to his hideous appearance; the denial of the love and acceptance he seeks metamorphoses the monster from an innocent creature into a murderous fiend. First, Victor Frankenstein, unwilling to take responsibility for the being to whom he gave life, flees from his monster in mortification and fear for creating not a beautiful new species but instead a horrifying beast. Like his creator, the first villagers the monster encounters do not attempt to communicate with him but immediately shun him in fear of his deformities. Then, the monster spends months learning from and benevolently assisting the virtuous De Lacey family, but despite his best efforts, the family rejects him on sight before he is able to demonstrate his noble intentions. The monster's last hope for acceptance and compassion lies in a female with the same defects as himself, and only Frankenstein possesses the ability to create such a being. In exchange for the monster's promise to live in peace with mankind, Frankenstein agrees to create a female, but the grotesqueness of his work prompts him to tear the body to pieces while the monster looks on. The creature considers this final act of rejection unforgivable; as his last hope of happiness shatters with the rending of the female's body, the monster vows eternal revenge on the man who carelessly gave him life only to withhold the means to enjoy it.

## Works Cited

Bloom, Harold. Introduction. *Mary Shelley*. Ed. Harold Bloom. Modern Critical Views. New York: Chelsea, 1985. 1-10.

Brooks, Peter. "'Godlike Science/Unhallowed Arts': Language, Nature, and Monstrosity." *Mary Shelley*. Ed. Harold Bloom. Modern Critical Views. New York: Chelsea, 1985.

Nelson, Lowry, Jr. "Night Thoughts on the Gothic Novel." *Mary Shelley*. Ed. Harold Bloom. Modern Critical Views. New York: Chelsea, 1985.

Shelley, Mary. *Frankenstein*. New York: Bantam, 1991.

## Sample 2: Final Draft

Blazing Down the Trail Towards Isonomy

"Lift Every Voice and Sing," by James Weldon Johnson, fervently conveys the valiant spirit of the African-American race in a moving and impassioned prose while delineating an equality-driven present, hardship-ridden past, and a promising future. The opening of the poem affirms that the existent tribulations the black American encounters will not hinder their aspirations for consonance among the diversified masses, as the African-American community marches defiantly down an unfamiliar path as an unbreakable entity. As Johnson's poem unfolds, the African-Americans' consciousness of their ancestors' laborious struggles incites animosity towards the white man while motivating their unfaltering determination to achieve racial equality. The final stanza emanates a serene aura as the afflictions hampering the oppressed fade into the distance and an enduring faith in the Supernatural grants them the audacity to persevere towards a transcendent union with God and all mankind. In order to uplift the spirits of a disheartened people, James Weldon Johnson, through the use of potent diction, connotative rhyming techniques, and momentous repetition, collimates the societal progression of the black American to an obstacle-ridden journey, tracing the present, past, and future in his inspirational poetic work, "Lift Every Voice and Sing."

The opening stanza of the poem establishes the persistence and vehemence coalescing within a discriminated, yet undeterred race to achieve vast unity encompassing all humanity, while likening the present to a joyous song ringing out down the trek towards universal equality. Johnson illustrates the intrepid willpower of black Americans to consummate a renowned societal status, equal to that of those who oppress them, through his conscientious word selection that projects an optimistic aura as they travel along an adversarial path. This efficacious use of potent diction propagates a sense of harmony and strength, delineating a connection between formidable words and an unyielding entity propelling forward: "Let it resound loud as the rolling sea" (6). The sea signifies an all-encompassing body into which the African-Americans assimilate, affirming the intent for a unified human race, which further impels their powerful cries for the Nation to cease bigoted treatment toward their race. Jane Tolbert-Rouchaleau, the distinguished author of *Black Americans of Achievement: James Weldon Johnson*, expounds on the author's use of stimulating wording:

> The lyrics inspired generations to dream of a time when blacks and whites could sit down together in friendship and understanding and be treated as equal citizens. People of all different races found encouragement in these lyrics and lifted their voices to echo the sentiments expressed in the anthem. (15)

The uplifting words trigger the long-awaited release of suppressed emotions by not only black Americans, but also white Americans, instituting a general sense of fellowship among the races. Furthermore, the concluding lines of the poem encapsulate the unwavering optimism of a fortified people, unfettered by the gloomy past in their pursuit of liberty and continuing a rhythmic, emboldened progression when Johnson exclaims: "Sing a song full of the faith that the dark past has taught us,/Sing a song full of the hope that the present has brought us,/Facing the rising sun of our new day begun/Let us march on till victory is won" (7-10). The author manifests an atmosphere of vigor and vitality, stemming from the triumph over past hardships and the spirit of hope stirring within the race, which is ideal for thrusting the race over discriminatory barriers and rousing them to boldly face the societal challenges impeding their journey. Tolbert-Rouchaleau analyzes Johnson's emphasis on reviving African-American consciousness of their outstanding potential as a dynamic force, asserting that, "He [Johnson] was intent on 'hammering at white America,' but he knew that for racial equality to be achieved 'it would be necessary to awaken black America'" (67). A revolutionary transformation of African-American conceptions regarding their dishonorable treatment and the surrounding implications is unnecessary; however, slight shifts and adjustments in the mental approach to rectifying racial transgressions must occur in order for a successful progression to ensue. Johnson's foundation of *The Daily American* provides the African-American community with an instrument to assert the tribulations that consume their daily lives: "...the newspaper became a voice against racial injustice and encouraged black advance-ment..." (*James*...1). *The Daily American*, the first African-American-driven newspaper, bestows upon the prejudiced an unprecedented opportunity to express their emotional distress while subconsciously unifying the race and solidifying their movement toward the ultimate goal of racial amity. Johnson's poem, "Lift Every Voice and Sing," exemplifies the African-American sentiment of the early twentieth-century, arising from the provocations befalling the race not only in the present, but in the latter-day as well.

As the work progresses, an anamnesis of the past unfolds, affirming the arduous toils that mark the African-American path and the deep-rooted indignation that fuels their determined course towards racial advancement. Through a scrupulous compilation of rhyming techniques and picturesque images, Johnson reinforces the depiction of the present social and past physical struggles hampering the African-American community. The rhyme scheme collimates the African-American cultural evolvement, and subsequently, the notorious encumbrances that mark the path previously tread by their progenitors: "Lift every voice and sing/Till earth and heaven ring,/Ring with the harmonies of Liberty;/Let our rejoicing rise/high as the listening skies,/Let it resound loud as the rolling sea" (1-6). Within the initial lines of the first stanza, two rhyming couplets present contentment as the final word of each line harmoniously agrees; thereafter, the cadence is disrupted as a rhythmically dissimilar line severs the couplet and breaks the accord. Likewise, society constructs internal and external hindrances, which periodically interrupt intervals of complacency along the African-American journey. In his analysis of James Weldon Johnson's expansive works, Robert E. Fleming, a highly regarded professor of English and expert on nineteenth-and twentieth-century literature, asserts the immense importance of the rhyme scheme, stating, "...the form and subject matter of his poems are characteristic of the period in which he wrote; that is, they are written...in rhymed verse, and they address subjects that are either the conventional subject matter of the poet or the specialized subject matter of the Afro-American poet" (42). Fleming concludes that the meticulous weaving of rhyming couplets interwoven with discordant lines yields powerful connotations; more specifically, the rhyme scheme alludes that the words themselves transcend the realm of composition and signify abstract ideas. Additionally, Johnson chronicles an acrimonious reflection on the tribulations of past generations that torment those of the present and exhort an injunction for the worldly transformation of discriminatory sentiments, stating, "Stony the road we trod/Bitter the chastening rod," (11-12). As each day bears unforeseen difficulties, the African-American community commemorates those of their ancestors, which includes the white man's perception of beneficial disciplinary action; for instance, the flogging that accompanies the evil institution of slavery, consequently, leads the black man to retain a bitter conception of the Anglo-Saxon race. Also throughout his poem, Johnson propagates the notion that, despite the torment of their forebears, the African-American people should no longer wallow in grief but instead embrace their intense power as an unflinching force, stating, "...the race should learn from their 'dark past,' should preserve in its faith in God and the nation, and should never cease to press toward its eventual victory" (Fleming 45). Johnson declares that the subjugated race should employ their faith in God, who perpetually imparts strength and guidance; thus, allowing the race to progress with every footstep and overcome challenges with every stride, never permitting sinister historical events to dissuade their efforts. Furthermore, the antagonistic conditions impressing the younger black American generations fuel Johnson's zealous poetic dedication toward racial advancement:

> It was during his college years that he first became aware of the depth of the racial problem in the United States, and Johnson's experience teaching black school children in a poor district of rural Georgia during two summers left a deep impression on him. The struggles and aspirations of American blacks form a central theme in the thirty or so poems that Johnson wrote as a student. (*James*...1)

Johnson acknowledges that the turmoil of preceding generations bears upon the innocent children of modernity as they unjustly suffer from the social afflictions arising predominantly from the racial climate of slavery. Johnson aspires to ameliorate these injustices through his impassioned quest for unencumbered equality, stimulating young black Americans to enrich the future of the race.

The concluding lines of the poem parallel the completion of a journey, conveying a harmonious projection of the future in which the oppressed derive a sense of protection from a beacon of hope that guides them to their ultimate destination: the transcendent union of mankind. Johnson inspires the persecuted to blaze down an obstacle-ridden trail consisting of maledict intentions and woeful expectations from a self-proclaimed superior race. The final lines of the poem utilize repetition to solidify the message of the African-American community, affirming that they subsist as an unswayable force, immoveable from their location on the path:

"True to our God/True to our native land" (32–33). The presence of repetition in these two lines inculcates the African-American drive toward isonomy as they persevere in their equality-bound propulsion, never retroceding, in utter anticipation of demonstrating to the white man that a conglomerated human race shares in the ownership of American soil. Dr. Hazel Arnett Ervin, a leading expert on the Harlem Renaissance, clarifies Johnson's manifestation of a unified black American society through the use of repetitious elements: "Most discussed by Johnson are what he calls the 'structural togetherness'...and 'repetition(s)' of spirituals and ragtime that made their way into the structure of African American poetry." (3). Johnson articulates that the use of repetitious diction in a poetic work solidifies the structural content and promulgates a firm message to the African-American people; moreover, repetition signifies their harmonious union as a race in accordance with the immovable position they procure on the path. Furthermore, the afflicted persons seek refuge and consolation in God, who ensures their continuity on the path and renders them the fortitude to prevail; thus, substantiating that the destiny of mankind is unobstructed unification: "Thou has brought us thus far on the way;/Thou who has by thy might/Led us into the light,/Keep us forever in the path, we pray" (24-27). In these lines, Johnson acknowledges that without God's advocacy of their cause, the black Americans would not possess the valor to voice the adversity continually deterring their envisions of equality. The community implores eternal solace in the kindling arms of their guardian, who symbolizes the equalizing force in the quest for racial fellowship. The coalescence of the black and white races will undoubtedly imprint an indelible mark on the heart of America, as Jane Tolbert-Rouchaleau elucidates:

> Convinced that natural and inevitable forces would help blacks become part of 'the American race of the future,' he [Johnson] predicted that the black man 'will fuse his qualities with those of other groups in the making of the ultimate American people; and that he will add a tint to America's complexion and put a perceptible permanent wave in America's hair. (99-100)

Johnson's use of religious undertones projects an uplifting atmosphere, ideal for the facilitation of African-American endeavors toward racial advancement. The African-American citizenry, believing that an unjust history will not disintegrate, utilizes the present as a tool to launch the race into an extraordinary future. The boldness God infuses into the African-American race allows their progression to stand independent of the whites' perceptions as their strong sense of self propels them toward their ultimate destination:

> The articles Johnson produced over the next ten years tended to be conservative, combining a strong sense of racial pride with a deep rooted belief that blacks could individually improve their lot by means of self-education and hard work even before discriminatory barriers had been removed (*James*...2).

Sharing the inspiration Johnson emanates in his work, the black community develops and maintains a strong sense of self-worth, refusing to permit discrimination by the white man, who represses their efforts of achieving consonance among the races.

James Weldon Johnson identifies racial inequality and societal injustices in his sententious poem, "Lift Every Voice and Sing," while portraying the recipients of such maltreatment as a steadfast and empowered force, thrusting through the trenches and hurdling the impediments the white race subjects upon them. The initial stanza bespeaks a call to action, supplicating the aggrieved to uphold the quest for impartiality. Johnson precedes with a reflection on foregoing generations, recounting the emotional weariness and distress of a persecuted people which fuels their desire for societal retribution. The final stages of Johnson's poem convey the African-American community steadily approaching their destination, deriving solace and subtle urging from a Higher Being. A contemplative and stimulating poem, James Weldon Johnson's "Lift Every Voice and Sing" manifests the African-American prevailing on a rhythmical progression towards the fusion of all races.

# Works Cited

Ervin, Hazel Arnett. *African American Literary Criticism, 1773 to 2000.* New York: Twayne Publishers, 1999.

Fleming, Robert E. *James Weldon Johnson.* Boston: Twayne Publishers, 1987.

"James Weldon Johnson." *Exploring Poetry.* Gale Group Databases. 12 Feb. 2004 <http://www.galegroup.com/free_resources/poets/bio/johnson_j.htm>.

Johnson, James Weldon. "Lift Every Voice and Sing." Jill Diesman's Homepage. Ed. Jill Diesman. 6 Mar. 2004 <http://www.nku.edu/~diesmanj/johnson.html>.

Tolbert-Rouchaleau, Jane. *Black Americans of Achievement: James Weldon Johnson.* New York: Chelsea House Publishers, 1988.

# Transitional words and Phrases/Peer Editing Checklists

# Transitional Words and Phrases

**...To show location**

| | | | | |
|---|---|---|---|---|
| above | behind | by | into | outside |
| across | below | down | near | over |
| against | beneath | in back of | off | throughout |
| along | beside | in front of | onto | to the right |
| among | between | inside | on top of | under |
| around | beyond | | | |

**...To show time**

| | | | | |
|---|---|---|---|---|
| about | first | meanwhile | soon | then |
| after | second | today | later | next |
| at | third | tomorrow | afterward | as soon as |
| before | till | next week | immediately | when |
| during | until | yesterday | finally | |

**...To compare two things**

| | | |
|---|---|---|
| in the same way | likewise | as |
| similarly | like | also |

**...To contrast things**

| | | | |
|---|---|---|---|
| but | otherwise | on the other hand | although |
| however | yet | still | even though |

**...To emphasize a point**

| | | |
|---|---|---|
| again | truly | for this reason |
| to repeat | in fact | to emphasize |

**...To conclude or summarize**

| | | | |
|---|---|---|---|
| as a result | finally | therefore | lastly |

**...To add information**

| | | | |
|---|---|---|---|
| again | another | for instance | finally |
| also | and | moreover | as well |
| additionally | besides | next | along with |
| in addition | for example | | |

**...To clarify**

| | | |
|---|---|---|
| in other words | for instance | that is |

# Graphic Organizer: Topic and Research Papers

## Graphic Organizer for Topic Paper

### Introduction/Thesis paragraph

| Identify author, title and topic | Refine topic | Identify first sub topic | Identify second sub topic | Identify third sub topic | Identify practical application |
|---|---|---|---|---|---|

| Body Paragraph One | Body Paragraph Two | Body Paragraph Three |
|---|---|---|
| Restate subtopic one | Restate subtopic two | Restate subtopic three |
| Refine topic | Refine topic | Refine topic |
| Introduce Quote | Introduce Quote | Introduce Quote |
| Quote | Quote | Quote |
| Comment on Quote | Comment on Quote | Comment on Quote |
| Introduce Quote | Introduce Quote | Introduce Quote |
| Quote | Quote | Quote |
| Comment on Quote | Comment on Quote | Comment on Quote |
| Introduce Quote | Introduce Quote | Introduce Quote |
| Quote | Quote | Quote |
| Comment on Quote | Comment on Quote | Comment on Quote |

### Conclusion

| Restate practical application | Restate and revisit strongest arguments |
|---|---|

## Graphic Organizer for Research Paper

**Introduction/Thesis paragraph**

| Identify author, title, and topic | Refine topic | Identify first subtopic | Identify second subtopic | Identify third subtopic | Identify practical application |
|---|---|---|---|---|---|

| **Body Paragraph 1** | **Body Paragraph 2** | **Body Paragraph 3** |
|---|---|---|
| Introduce subtopic 1 | Introduce subtopic 2 | Introduce subtopic 3 |
| Refine subtopic | Refine subtopic | Refine subtopic |
| Introduce primary quote | Introduce primary quote | Introduce primary quote |
| Primary quote | Primary quote | Primary quote |
| Comment on quote | Comment on quote | Comment on quote |
| Introduce secondary quote | Introduce secondary quote | Introduce secondary quote |
| Secondary quote | Secondary quote | Secondary quote |
| Comment on quote | Comment on quote | Comment on quote |
| Introduce primary quote | Introduce primary quote | Introduce primary quote |
| Primary quote | Primary quote | Primary quote |
| Comment on quote | Comment on quote | Comment on quote |
| Introduce secondary quote | Introduce secondary quote | Introduce secondary quote |
| Secondary quote | Secondary quote | Secondary quote |
| Comment on quote | Comment on quote | Comment on quote |
| Introduce primary quote | Introduce primary quote | Introduce primary quote |
| Primary quote | Primary quote | Primary quote |
| Comment on quote | Comment on quote | Comment on quote |

**Conclusion**

| Restate practical application | Restate strongest points from subtopics. |
|---|---|

# Grading Rubrics and Peer Editing Checklists

## Research Paper Checklist

Brainstorming Notes (1 page) = 5 points → these may be handwritten
Outline (1 page minimum) = 5 points → proper form: GT, I, II, III, Conc.
Thesis Paragraph = 5 points → author, title, GT, 3 subtopics, T Statement
Topic Paper (2 pages minimum) = 5 points → T Par. 3 body paragraphs/9 quotes & Conc.
Annotated Bibliography #1 = 5 points → Quotes, body paragraph, photocopies
Annotated Bibliography #2 = 5 points → Quotes, body paragraph, photocopies
Annotated Bibliography #3 = 5 points → Quotes, body paragraph, photocopies
Rough Draft (+ Works Cited) = 5 points → 5 paragraphs, PSPSP, form & content

**TOTAL =**       **40 points** Forty of 100 points are earned for turning in all required stages leading up to the Final Draft. However, a full 5 points can only be earned if each stage is written according to set guidelines as outlined in the *Tao of Composition/MLA Handbook*. Thus, if the Topic Paper has been edited by only 2 people instead of the required 3, or the Outline is only ¾ of a single page, you will receive less than 5 points. Annotated Bibliographies **MUST** have photocopied Secondary Sources stapled to the back before any points are received.

**ALL** stages, except Brainstorming Notes, **MUST** be edited and signed by at least three people, be they students, parents, teachers; signatures are proof of their attempt to edit your work.

*       *       *

<u>Final Draft Checklist</u>
The remaining 60 possible points will be divided into two sections: 30 points for Form/Structure and 30 points for Content. Form/Structure is one's accuracy in the physical presentation of one's paper; this includes but is not limited to: margins, block quote set up and proper citations. Content is one's ability to clearly and coherently present one's research findings. Below are all the components of an outstanding Final Draft in Form/Structure and Content.

## Form/Structure

- ➤ 1-inch margins all the way around except for last name and page # in upper right-hand corner and around block quotes

- ➤ last name and page # in upper right-hand corner is ½-inch from top of page

- ➤ block quotes are 2 inches in from the side and justified on left and right sides; single spacing is preferred, although double is not incorrect; there are no quotation marks around block quotes

- ➤ proper MLA heading on first page

- ➤ title is not bolded or underlined, etc.

- ➤ 12-point Times New Roman

- ➤ Citations: proper MLA → for example "...is purely a Promethean character" (Jones 57).

- ➤ Quotes within Body Paragraphs must follow P-S-P-S-P format

- ➤ Quotes must be introduced with more than the author's last name and the word "states"

- ➤ As for the Thesis Paragraph, within the first two lines, we must have the General Topic + the author and title of the Primary Source (which should be underlined or in italics)

- ➤ The Thesis Paragraph must also contain three distinct Subtopics, preferably each with its own sentence or two

- ➤ The Thesis Paragraph must conclude with a Thesis Statement summarizing the importance of your Subtopics to the General Topic while providing a transition into the first Body Paragraph

- ➤ Present Tense unless within quotes

- ➤ No rhetorical questions

- ➤ Pronoun agreement; anytime "their" is used, double check the prior pronoun to make sure it agrees

- ➤ Obviously, check for grammatical and spelling and usage errors

## Content

- ➤ In the Thesis Paragraph, three Subtopics must be clear and distinct and flow smoothly from one to the next.

- ➤ The opening sentence of the Thesis Paragraph must introduce the General Topic as well as the author and title of the Primary Source in a clear, vivid manner so that there is no misunderstanding or ambiguity as to what one is discussing

- ➤ Body Paragraphs must provide support for the three clear and distinct Subtopics with a variety of sentence structures

- ➤ Quotes must not only support the general theme of one's Subtopics, but they must also move the information along, not reiterate what you've already said in analysis; quotes are not meant to repeat information, they are meant to enhance analysis

- ➤ Speaking of analysis, sufficient analysis must be provided after each quote and before the next quote; one cannot simply go from quote to quote and pretend that's analysis

- ➤ In the Conclusion, no new evidence or information is allowed; summarize one's main points in 4-6 sentences

- ➤ Overall, Content can best be described as the ability to delve into one's General Topic and Subtopics while providing insightful analysis that's clear, comprehensive, profound, and focused.

- ➤ Outstanding Content is enhanced for the reader through the use of excellent transitional words and phrases

## Research Paper:
## Peer Editing Checklist

Whose research paper is being graded: _____

Who is grading this research paper: _____

          ❋                        ❋                        ❋

Circle the grade deserved, 1 being the lowest and 5 the highest, then mark this grade on the right-hand side. The "Points" column will allow you to tally the initial 40 points.

Brainstorming Notes (1 page)  ... 1 ... 2 ... 3 ... 4 ... 5     Points: _____
Outline (1 page minimum)  ... 1 ... 2 ... 3 ... 4 ... 5     Points: _____
Thesis Paragraph  ... 1 ... 2 ... 3 ... 4 ... 5     Points: _____
Topic Paper (2 pages min.)  ... 1 ... 2 ... 3 ... 4 ... 5     Points: _____
Annotated Bibliography #1  ... 1 ... 2 ... 3 ... 4 ... 5     Points: _____
Annotated Bibliography #2  ... 1 ... 2 ... 3 ... 4 ... 5     Points: _____
Annotated Bibliography #3  ... 1 ... 2 ... 3 ... 4 ... 5     Points: _____
Rough Draft  ... 1 ... 2 ... 3 ... 4 ... 5     Points: _____

Total Points: _____

          ❋                        ❋                        ❋

## Peer Editing Checklist

Form/Structure and Content comprise the remaining 60 points at 30 points per section. On a prior sheet, you were given the parameters to satisfy all 30 points for both sections. Based on those parameters, assign a number grade of up to 30 points for each section and place it in the appropriate space below. As well, provide an explanation as to why this paper received the grade you assigned. TAKE THIS TASK SERIOUSLY.

Form/Structure                    Points: _____

Content                           Points: _____

TOTAL POINTS: _____

0-595-28438-8

Made in the USA
Lexington, KY
16 October 2011